BUSINESSMAN'S
HANDBOOK

BUSINESSMAN'S HANDBOOK

by

Lloyd Cole

Everything to help the newcomer

in business to succeed

MAIDENHEAD

First published 1993

First paperback edition 1994
94 95 96 97 6 5 4 3 2 1

Lloyd Cole
37 College Avenue,
Maidenhead, SL6 6AZ, UK

ISBN
1 87405225 5 hbk
1 87405227 1 pbk

A record of the cataloguing in publication data
is available from the Bitish Library

Printed in Finland by WSOY

CONTENTS

INTRODUCTION

The aim of this book is to enable the man or woman entering the business world to succeed. The self employed owner and the manager of a company both need certain qualities to ensure they will make a good job of running the business. Learning by studying is a lot less costly than learning by experience.

Chapters deal with starting a business, deciding objectives and acting to realise those objectives by acquiring management skills.

Considerable thought is given to relations with staff and customers, to how to improve the business, and to details such as credit control. There is a chapter devoted to marketing and sales, so vital to the good health of any enterprise.

Every manager should be well equipped for the battle ahead and on the field of industrial and commercial battles the only sin is ignorance.

This book will help the young manager, small business owner and young executive to avoid the pitfalls surrounding all risk taking and to be well on the way to understanding the secrets of business success.

1

STARTING A BUSINESS

When starting a business it is important to consider all the possible problems that may be encountered. Learning by experience is the most costly way of learning anything. Far better to learn from the experience of others. There are training courses based on experience and there are books like this one that may well acquaint you with the answers to the many difficulties, and at a much lower cost than by trial and error. If it is best to learn from experience why not send learner drivers out on their own to experiment? Nothing could be more costly.

Consider everything that may arise before you start. Know the district in which you intend to trade. Know the availability of staff and supplies. Know the current state of the trade you intend to enter. Find out why others ceased trading in the same business or in the same area. Know as much as you can before you venture forth. Learn before you pay for unfortunate experience. Well taught in advance is the same as well equipped for the future. Why be blind when you can see? Why skid in a car when you can learn how to avoid skidding?

There is little point in falling to your death from a

mountain because you felt it sufficient to learn from experience. Listen first to what experienced climbers have to say. Buy the right equipment. Obey the rules. Remember it is much cheaper to learn from the experience of others, and there are many books and courses to help the beginner.

This does not mean that there is no room for innovation and new ideas. It means that the possible problems should be understood before commencing on a new venture. Once aware of the pitfalls there may be room for a new approach to overcoming the difficulties.

In establishing any new business it is vital that lines of supply are known to exist. The manufacturer must be able to obtain his basic supplies from which to make his lines. He should be sure of constant and sufficient supply. It is quite useless to make and promote a new line only to find that you cannot get enough raw materials to fulfil the orders. For the same reason it is important to be able to recruit the right kind of staff in the numbers required.

Staying with the subject of supply, you should not advertise something that you are unable to supply. Also consider the need to maintain supplies at a consistent price. No new business can afford to find itself having to increase prices too soon after launching a product. The maintenance of prices over a reasonable period is of some importance. It is also likely to prove an obstacle to real success if one creates a demand that cannot then be met in a reasonable time.

Therefore in establishing a new business make sure of sources of raw materials in the quantities likely to be needed and at a consistent price for a reasonable time. At the same time be aware of the possible availability of staff.

Be aware of the possible changes in the market for the goods you intend to produce and/or sell. Do not enter a market that is about to die. If in a retail field try to discover any possible changes likely to take place in the area. Do not open a school uniform supply shop in a district about to lose its main school! Do not open a road café in the centre of a town or village about to be bypassed. Get hold of all the information you can on conditions prevailing or about to prevail in the area in which you intend to operate.

Not only should you consider the possibility of a dying demand for your product, consider also the prospect of a new market about to materialise, and get in first. Anticipation is a pre-requisite for outstanding success in a new business. In this and in many other ways knowledge is indeed power, and such power increases the potential for success.

Anticipation helps to make a good driver on the roads, and lack of anticipation can mean an accident and possibly death. The same applies to a business. Before commencing a business, survey the territory and consider the prospects as fully as you can. Remember what happens to fools that rush in. Prepare well and prosper. It is better to sell an item at a price that can be maintained because of demand, than to offer something at a cut price that nobody wants. Cheapness is not necessarily the secret for success. If you can sell cheaper because of the quantity you can sell, this is success.

Consider not only the area and the prospects in the area in which you intend to trade. Consider also what provision is already being made in the market you are about to enter. If a great deal is already on offer you will need a compelling reason why your product should find a market. This could be the price, or quality, or superior marketing. Consider everything. Have a policy that has been thought through.

Consider whether it is best to make an item or to have

this item made for you. In either case, ensure supply.

- There is no substitute for thorough preparation.

In manufacturing and distribution it is important to be able to obtain the staff needed. Consider whether it would be better to employ full or part time staff, or both. Also, in some cases, one should consider the use of home workers. This can greatly reduce the cost of premises, and the use of part time or home workers can mean that labour can be varied with demand at much lower cost.

In other words, keep constant day-by-day costs to a minimum consistent with the ability to produce the amount of goods required as and when they are needed.

In manufacturing or large wholesale distribution consider the likelihood of disruption by the local workforce. Many businesses recently established in Britain have been opened in areas where there is a history of good labour relations. Some areas have failed to attract new business because of their poor record of industrial unrest. This is an important consideration.

In setting up any business the possibility of theft by staff must be considered. Reasonable and thorough security is vital. Not only must the business be protected from theft, but also from incompetence of staff. To have incompetent or even unpleasant staff can mitigate greatly against the success of a business. It is essential that only really competent staff are employed in top positions, but in contact with your customers they must be agreeable and pleasant.

- Staff must be able, loyal and pleasant.

Do not overlook the need for good sales staff. Whether dealing with the public or with the trade, remember that sales are the lifeblood of a business. There are no profits without sales. Later, I will devote a whole chapter to the subject.

In considering sales it is important to consider the terms on which sales are made. Any fool can give his goods away. A business must have sensible credit control. When making something, or marketing something made by others, there is no profit if the goods concerned are not paid for. A good margin of profit does not exist if no payment is made.

This is one reason why good competent staff are essential, and good credit control absolutely vital. If you sell goods that are not paid for, you not only lose the cost of the goods but also the cost of the selling of the goods.

- A good salesman gets good orders from good payers.

Added to the cost of producing goods must be the cost of obtaining payment for them. Every extra statement sent out adds to costs and reduces profit. Allowance for bad debts can be included in the total cost of a product before deciding a selling price, and in this way a certain amount of bad debt can be carried without loss. However if this means a higher price than necessary for the goods sold, you may be undercut by a company with better credit control who does not have to make allowances for bad debts. All sales are not good sales. Goods are only sold where payment is certain. If payment is not forthcoming, the goods have been given away, not sold.

In founding a new business it is important to know what is already being done. A competitor's price should be noted. This can then be undercut, or better quality can be offered at the same price. New ideas can be incorporated or better guarantees given.

Having made sure of supplies, arranged appropriate

staff, made or bought in the best possible product or range of goods to retail or wholesale, the next consideration is to have a competitive price, and to consider your sales plan and organisation. While very large orders from one customer are very pleasant to receive, it is not always wise to put all your eggs in one basket. If you do and the basket upsets, you have nothing left, and other potential customers may have been offended as a result of your ignoring them in favour of the big account. It will, in most cases, be best to have more than one supplier and as wide a range of customers as possible.

- Very few businesses make a success of having only one customer.

There are certain precautions that should be considered. There are many misfortunes that should be insured against. Be wise and cover yourself against everything possible. You can insure against fire and theft at least, and whatever the cost, insurance is cheaper than catastrophe.

Study constantly what is going on around you, especially if in the retail business. A movement of people away from a district can make a considerable difference to the buying policy of a business. Be ready for change always, and never be afraid of change. Better change than perish.

It may be wise under certain circumstances to combine with a competitor. Be prepared always to do what is best for your business. Try to anticipate the need for change. Have a good idea in mind what you will do in any given circumstance.

Plan ahead as far as you can. Get in good management to carry out your plans with enthusiasm and competence. If you intend to run a one person affair make sure you have studied ahead sufficiently to be competent yourself. There is no substitute for able management.

There is one more important consideration at the commencement of a business, that of finance. Without ample finance you may not be able to succeed, however competent. Competence will lead to the proper use of finance but will not necessarily take its place.

- Whatever finance you have been able to arrange, you must work within its limitations.

A clever person will be able to make money go further, but there will be limits beyond which there is danger.

To arrange enough capital it is necessary to have plans that look viable to an investor or a bank. This re-emphasises the need for planning ahead and for a thorough knowledge of what you intend to do; how you intend to overcome problems; and the reasonable prospects for the business. People who have money to invest usually ask lots of questions. They will not invest in you if you cannot answer the questions to their satisfaction. After all, why should they? If you cannot say how you expect to succeed you will not appear to be offering a sound proposition.

One way of managing on existing capital, and doing without (perhaps) a costly loan or investment, would be by managing with a smaller staff, or with a greater proportion of part time staff, or by installing labour-saving equipment. When recession or depression hits a country it is found that many businesses and government departments can run quite satisfactorily on a smaller staff.

- To be top heavy with administrative staff is a sure way to failure in business.

To repeat myself again: know the problems, study the methods of dealing with them, and avoid the pitfalls.

A further consideration regarding finance is how you are going to pay for it. If you have to borrow money, work out how you can pay the interest and how you can eventually repay the loan. You must be able to earn enough profit to pay the regular expenses of the business plus the interest on the loan. The amount of profit that would cover basic expenses and give a small income might not cover the extra cost involved in borrowing to finance growth. It is essential to ensure that profits will cover all expenses.

If you cannot pay all the expenses necessary from the maximum profits you can make while remaining competitive, you should not proceed any further.

Once you have made sure of supplies, staff and finance you must decide on the organisation of your business, whether to run the business entirely yourself or to take a partner, or to form a limited company. There are advantages and drawbacks with all methods of operation.

To trade on your own as a self-employed owner of a business has many points in its favour. Apart from anything else, you have no-one else to answer to! You back your own judgement, and enjoy the thrill of building your own empire. Also, you do not have to share your profits with anyone else. In starting a business on your own, getting started is very easy. You just start. Being the sole authority means quick action. Many suppliers will give more credit to a sole trader than to a limited liability company. There are tax advantages in being self employed. You probably become a friend of your staff and your customers with whom you have a one-to-one relationship.

The principal drawback to sole proprietorship is the unlimited liability that goes with it. If you have borrowed money from a bank and given your home as security, and things go badly wrong, you can lose your home as well as your business. You can be made bankrupt by your creditors and end up losing all your assets.

As far as growth of the business is concerned you are limited to what you can plan and attain by yourself. There is also the well-known concept that two heads are better than one. Also the combined capital of two people might just be enough to properly finance the enterprise.

There are of course disadvantages in partnerships. It is difficult to work well with shared ownership. Partners do not always agree. Dissolving a partnership can kill off a business.

The forming of a limited company has the advantage of limiting the liability of the directors, and if the business collapses directors do not lose personal assets except in cases of proven fraud.

There are different ways of starting in business. You can just start, which may well be the most fun. Starting from nothing with a good idea is an adventure worth undertaking. There is nothing like it, providing you are not too timid. You need courage and belief in yourself. You may have a good head start because you have found a hole in the market that nobody is filling. You may have an idea of how something already being done can be done better. It may be that certain businesses in a trade have become complacent and you have heard the complaints against this situation and feel that you can offer a more vital and comprehensive service. It often happens that somebody comes from nowhere and takes over a trade from many well-founded competitors. This is done by enthusiasm and by listening to what people want. The older, established firms have become deaf and the newcomer has ears and eyes open to all the possibilities.

If you are of a more cautious nature, you may want to buy an existing business rather than undertake the building of a business from scratch. You may feel happier taking over a business that has already gone through the pangs of birth. To my mind, this is a very expensive way of going into business. However, if you have the necessary capital, buying a business can be a most successful way of entering a market. You need to know what you are doing. You must know the pitfalls that dog the feet of those thinking of buying a business. You must be aware of the tricks that a dishonest seller may be prepared to perpetrate against an unwary buyer.

- Remember that the buyer must beware.

Thinking of retailing as a business, I have direct experience of what happened to a buyer of a gift shop. A lady bought a gift shop and all its stock from a couple who had always been regarded as honest and honourable people. However, when one of the main suppliers of jewellery items called on the shop he found the new owners were selling items from his company for at least twice the normal retail price. The new owner was finding sales very poor indeed. It turned out that the seller had doubled all the prices just before the sale and then offered the stock at 50 per cent discount. This meant that the new buyer was paying not the trade price but the actual retail price. She had been told that these prices could be doubled for retail sale. This meant the new owner was trying to sell at twice the price the shop had previously charged. She had been deceived and cheated into paying twice the price any trade buyer should have paid. It was made to look good by the offering of a 50 per cent discount on all the stock. This was a very nasty swindle. Let the buyer beware.

This example demonstrates that nobody should buy a business unaware of the normal trade and retail price of the stock being taken over. It should be a fairly easy matter to check prevailing retail prices in other shops. Also, one could always check prices with the previous owner's suppliers, or with other possible suppliers.

I think it necessary to say that nobody should buy into a business without reasonable pre-knowledge of price prevailing in that particular trade. The lady mentioned in the example had to lose over £10,000 on stock that had to be sold for half the price she had paid for it. On top of this, a great deal of the stock was old and was not even worth half the price paid. It is doubtful if a great deal of the stock was worth one fifth of the price paid. No informed buyer would be caught by such dishonest sellers.

There is no substitute for knowledge of the trade you are about to enter. No buyer of a business should go in blind. A reasonable knowledge of the trade concerned is essential *before* purchasing. Learning by experience can be very costly indeed, and it is not the right way to enter business. To buy too quickly and in ignorance is to repent over quite a considerable loss. Not only will such an ignorant buyer lose money, but this loss may make survival impossible. Making a success of a new business is hard enough without imposing unnecessary handicaps on oneself. Do not be a fool, for a fool and his money are soon parted!

Requirement number one, before buying a new business, is therefore a reasonable up-to-date knowledge of prices prevailing in the trade. Also, if considering a gift shop, or any business involved in fashion, it is important to know what is old stock.

- Old stock should be bought very cheaply or not at all.

A buyer of an existing business should size up how the prospective purchase compares with others in the same

area. Is it in as good a position or is its position secondary
to a competitor who is likely to fulfil most of the demand? Is
the shop modern and light or is it dark and dismal giving the
impression that not much business is expected? Is it easy to
come into the shop and buy? Are things well laid out or is
the shop cluttered? Can you talk to some local people to
find out the reputation of the shop? Are you going to have
to work hard to win back lost customers? If it seems that
the business has been failing there is no good will to pay
for. You should pay considerably less if in fact you are going
to have to re-establish a failing enterprise. Remember I am
now considering retail trading. In this connection it is
important to compare the business with any competition.
Also, it is vital to consider customer relationships. Is it a
happy shop with contented staff and customers who love to
come in for a chat?

Consider how good or bad the buying has been. A look
at the stock will tell you if the buying has been competent.
Are the right things being stocked for the people around the
shop? Are the more likely customers young or old? Wealthy
or poor? And is the shop stocked with the right goods for
the neighbourhood?

Bearing in mind the example quoted earlier, check that
prices on goods have not been raised to an unjustifiable
level. You are the buyer. It is your money that is at risk. Do
not give your money away.

Quite apart from whether the stock is up-to-date,
consider if it is fast or slow moving stock? You are investing
in the stock. How long can you afford to wait for good
returns? This consideration makes a difference to what you
should pay for different stock or even if you should refuse
to buy some stock at all. Again, it is your money. Do not be
so afraid of not getting the business you think you want that

you finish up paying more than you should. Pay only what the assets of the business are worth. This is not necessarily what they cost, for you do not have to pay for other people's inefficient buying. Do not be too influenced by what the seller says the attainable profit margin is. This is often suggested by the offer of 50 per cent off the shop's retail prices. This is only a satisfactory price if the shop price is what it should be and all the goods are up-to-date. Even then it is doubtful if you should pay 50 per cent of the shop price.

You must bear in mind the time you consider it will take to sell the stock. You must pay less for goods that will take two years to sell than for those that will go in two months.

It is not a bad idea to try and talk to the shop's suppliers. You can check if they have been paying accounts regularly to time. If it turns out that payments have been consistently very late then it is likely that the business is poor. If the seller has been telling you of booming business but the suppliers of stock have hardly ever been paid to time then it is likely that you are not getting the facts from the seller. It is possible that the seller has personal problems that have been taking the money but, generally, slow payment of accounts means the business is not too healthy. You should buy such a business only at the price to be paid for an unhealthy business not at the price to be paid for a booming store. Be careful. It is your money, so spend it wisely. Just as when you are buying in a shop for your own needs you should be seeking value for money. Anything less is a bad deal.

You have to be able to recoup your money in a reasonable time or it would be better to put the money into a savings account.

Goodwill is only of value if it has a future benefit. People talk about goodwill as if it exists just because the business existed, and when they come to sell a business they immediately ask for money for goodwill. However, many businesses have absolutely no goodwill at all! Requests for goodwill payment should be looked into carefully. Is there really any goodwill that will give future earning power?

- As a general principle the price you pay for any business must relate to what you can expect to earn.

You may be prepared to pay more than you need because you can see considerable profitable future business to be available. This is the crucial test. This is what matters. What can I earn from this business in the future? If it is going to be very difficult, or will take a long time to make a decent profit, then the buying price must be low. This applies equally to stock. The stock is not worth what it costs you if it is going to take a very long time to sell, if at all. Worth of stock and goodwill in the present can only be fully decided by reasonable future forecasts of profits.

It will always be worthwhile to find out why the seller is selling. It may be to escape from a money-losing business that is virtually worthless. Find out.

If you buy a good business you will benefit from the knowledge and expertise of the seller. This benefit is what makes it appropriate to pay for goodwill. A further reason for being willing to pay for goodwill is if you can see how to make more of the business than has previously been attained.

If all the costing in the business is wrong, and therefore profit of any kind is unlikely without major replanning, then there is no goodwill in that business.

When considering the purchase of an existing business work out how you can improve the business. Chapter 4 deals with improving a business so I will not deal with it now except to say that it is important to consider whether improvements can be made without too much expense immediately after finding the purchase price.

If you have considered everything and have decided to buy, check that you are sure what you should pay. Be aware of business trends in the area. Is a bypass coming which will take away all your passing trade? Is this why the seller is getting out of the business, because passing trade has been a major part of the turnover? Are the nearby schools closing and did the business rely on sales of school uniforms and other items bought by schoolchildren and their parents? Is a nearby bus-stop to be moved? Is Boots or WHSmith or Woolworth or another such large operator about to move away from nearby? Is the doctor's surgery about to move from next door to the next street? Find out what is going to happen. Ask people, until you are sure that nothing detrimental is about to happen.

As well as considering what may be happening in the neighbourhood you should also consider the trends in the trade concerned. Fashions change. Be sure you do not buy into a business that is just going out of favour. You need to be assured of long term prospects.

A great deal of the above applies only to retail businesses. There are one or two thoughts about manufacturing and wholesale businesses that are worth considering. In buying a manufacturing or wholesale business it is important to be sure that there is, or can easily be, good control of .costs. Also be sure there is, or can soon be, effective credit control. While looking at turnover figures check to see if they may have been achieved at too high a cost. Good management can of course turn round such a position. If the costs are too high the net profit will be too low. If a buyer can see how to achieve the same turnover with lower costs then it may well pay to buy a business that has not been run correctly.

If the business on offer has many bad debts then it may be possible to turn the low profits to large profits by decent, thorough credit control. Consider however the possibility that the goods have only sold in the quantities shown because they were virtually given away. Study the real worth of the goods being made or bought in.

Rights, trademarks and brand names will only have value if they will provide future good business. Again the price you can offer for a manufacturing or wholesale business is subject to the same limitations as if you were buying a retail store. You should pay only a sum related to what you can earn in the future. Again, if you are buying a good business you will be able to benefit from the experience and knowledge of the seller and his or her staff.

Again, in deciding whether to buy a business, consider if you can reasonably make more of the business once you take it over. You may need to consider if you can attain the same sales at less cost. Such would be the first step to making a success of your take-over.

All that has been said in this chapter amounts to the necessity of knowing the facts in every facet of business. Dickens wrote: 'Facts alone are wanted in life.'

There is no substitute for facts. Facts are firm and unchanging, as Browning wrote: 'Facts are facts, and flinch not.'

The successful manager seeks the facts as they are and for the future, as stated by George Curzon: 'Intelligent anticipation of facts, even before they occur.'

A successful owner of a business needs facts above all else. Without them there is no basis for working out the objectives of the business. A manager without facts is like a fish out of water. As Marlowe said: 'There is no sin but ignorance.'

Napoleon once remarked that 'England is a nation of shopkeepers.' Certainly there are plenty of shops. Some must fail for this reason. However, a good shopkeeper has much to be proud of. He must have mastered many problems to stay in business. He will have learned that turnover is not necessarily profitable.

- When starting in business make sure it is the kind of business that will suit you.If you want to be a manager of a business, enter a trade that you will be happy to be in.

While this book must of necessity deal mainly with large businesses I will give some attention to small businesses. In considering starting a small business you can choose something small enough to run yourself if that is what you want to do. If you intend introducing staff to do most of the work you must choose a business with enough potential.

- Consider that you must make more in profit that you could earn as a worker or the project is not worth launching.

2

POSSIBLE FAILURE

Later in this volume I will detail methods of survival and success. However, if failure has to be faced in difficult times, remember that all is not lost while opportunities for survival remain. There are several possibilities worth consideration.

One thing is certain. If you are trading as a self-employed person owning a business of your own, bankruptcy must be avoided because there is no worse enemy of yourself or your creditors than the official receiver. I have always felt that official *deceiver* would be a better title. It is worthwhile making every effort to convince creditors of this, for the official receiver is of little use to them. It is a scandal that the treatment meted out to a sincere person who has failed in running a business is so severe, while directors of limited companies are more protected. The independent small trader can be stripped of everything and the final position in relation to the trader's creditors is made worse by the selling of assets for next to nothing by the official receiver. In these circumstances I feel the most blameworthy party is the official receiver.

It should be possible to convince creditors that they are

likely to receive a greater part of what is due to them by leaving a business in the hands of its owner. Certain safeguards can be put into operation to protect creditors without killing a business that might be rescued with a little thought and application.

- Anything is to be preferred to the utter ruination brought about by the official receiver.

It has happened that in cases where the assets of a business were more or less equal to its debts, once the official receiver confiscates the assets the creditors will be lucky to get ten per cent of what they are owed.

It might well be that if creditors have received good trade from a debtor they might be willing to finance the continuance of the business. Why not? Providing that the failure of the business is a result of misfortune, mistakes or simply lack of capital, rather than fraudulent behaviour, then it might well pay the creditors to support and help the debtor. Why should creditors kill off a good customer?

In the event of possible failure a debtor should approach creditors with the proposition that they take a stake in the business to the advantage of all concerned. It has to be in the best interests of the creditors to keep a customer's assets out of the grasp of the official receiver. After all, with additional capital introduced into the business by the creditors they might well be creating a much improved sales outlet for their goods: and in the person of the debtor they may well have a very useful asset. The debtor in such circumstances might well prove a most useful colleague, and would have every reason to be grateful to his benefactors.

- It is important to realise that every business failure is not a rogue. That, in fact, very few failures are rogues.

- If the creditors are not interested in taking equity
perhaps the employees might be.

It could be worthwhile approaching the staff who might be willing to provide the finance needed to keep the business in existence, and along with it their jobs. Often a bank or finance house will support such an arrangement.

Let the motto be: never say die until dead! Try all possible means to keep a business alive. These are cases where people who have failed in business have later become captains of industry. It might be considered better if they had been saved from failure in the first place.

At the start of any business venture, certain matters should be attended to in order to attain a solid base for expansion and improvement. Certainly, a prospective manager or owner should collect all possible information on suppliers of either raw materials or finished goods that will be needed in the business. It is vital that the business is assured of supplies of the right materials of the right quality and quantity at the right time and at the right price.

- It is management's first duty to secure supply lines.

Arrangements must be made for adequate storage facilities. Supplies should be arranged so that no more storage space is required than is absolutely necessary, since it costs money to store. It is ridiculous to hold vast stocks in expensive premises for long periods, unless the reduction in price for buying the larger quantity is substantial. The saving in costs on the supplies should amount to more than the cost of the extra space needed over a period of twelve months. The other possible reason for holding large stocks for a long time is if there is a danger that the supplies may not continue to be readily available.

Once management has found out how long it takes to obtain supplies, stock can then be held in the quantity needed in that period plus a little more for emergencies. It is important not to take on any unnecessary expense.

- Too much stock is as big a mistake as too little stock.

At the commencement of a business, or perhaps a while before, sources of supplies that will be needed must be ascertained. There are numerous means of establishing who all the different sources are. With this information the businessman can go on to find out which source offers the best price and terms, and which is known to be most reliable.

- Perfect price plus consistent and totally reliable deliveries are the utopia of the business manager.

In searching for the best sources of supply the manager can study the promotional material sent out by the leading suppliers. This of course will be biased, but it can be followed up with a visit to the supplier. Much can be checked, and confirmed or otherwise, by such a visit. Also, it is possible to consult others who have used the supplier.

Much can be gleaned from reliable trade papers in which the editorial comment can usually be relied upon for accuracy. Trade directories are useful only insofar as they provide a list of names and addresses. Once you have compiled a list you can make calls on the potential suppliers or ask other traders about their suitability. It is always worthwhile finding out which suppliers are held in good esteem.

Both your own and the supplier's sales people will be able to give you information on suppliers. When sales people call on you it often becomes apparent whether they think well of their employer. This is often a clue to the sort of company represented. If the sales person is proud to work for the company and is convinced of its back-up and support, it is probable that it is a good company.

Visits to suppliers' premises or to exhibitions can be a considerable help in choosing the best suppliers for your purpose. Visiting premises is only a real help if you are free to check the stock available. At trade exhibitions there is an opportunity to see whole ranges at once. You can compare one range with another and the prices of each. You can ask about terms and service offered at each stand. Exhibitions can be a bit of a bore but they can also solve many problems. Often at an exhibition you will see people who might never contact you in any other way. You must do what is needed to ensure that you buy the best supplies at the best price, and that with the price you are also getting a certainty of good and dependable deliveries.

▪ As well as sources of supply a businessman must consider the availability and use of capital.

The best use of the money available is the art of good management. This ties in with finding the right suppliers. One of the points to consider in choosing a supplier is their delivery service. To make the best use of one's capital it is essential that the level of stock held should be the lowest that will do the job plus a small amount for emergencies. Good management means keeping stocks low and being able to rely on regular supplies of further stock just ahead of time, when needed to fulfil orders. All businesses benefit from pre-ordered supplies of stock; that means little or no overstocking. Let the supplier pay the costs of holding large stocks. Be certain the supplier will deliver as required.

The reason for caution in holding only a necessary

amount of stock is that the first law of modern business is survival. Many fail to survive because they overstock and then find that income is insufficient to pay for the extra stock.

As well as the quantity of stock to hold there is also the matter of price. If in order to have the delivery service you need you are asked too high a price, refuse to pay such a price. Argue that a good regular order entitles you to the very best service. Most suppliers will see the justice in this, especially if you negotiate with someone senior like the owner, a director or sales manager.

Price is important as a base from which to work. Once you are sure you have your cost price right there is much else to think about. While it is important at first to secure a basic cost it must then be remembered that price is only part of value for money. Very important too is quality.

- Nothing is cheap if it is no use for its purpose.

A cheap whistle that will not make a sound when blown is of no use whatsoever. The fact that it cost very little does not matter. Good management will obtain high quality at a competitive price. Anyone can buy cheap rubbish. In many businesses a better quality article is often little dearer that a sub-standard one. Do not be fooled by a low price for a low-grade article. At the same time do not be talked into paying an excessive amount to obtain reasonable quality. No good is no good however low the cost.

The right price for good quality will amount to a durable article. Quality and durability are twin requirements. A cheaper line can actually be dearer if quality and durability are overlooked. The high road to success is to be able to offer high quality with durability at an obviously reasonable price.

The man who complained that he could not understand how he became bankrupt because he was the cheapest in town, had obviously overlooked the necessity also to provide quality and durability.

The manager or owner of a new business must learn to know the business. It must be remembered that there is no worthwhile policy without thorough observation. It is essential in a business of any kind to obtain all the facts that will lead to considered decisions. When you have all the facts you can weigh one thing with another and decide the best course of action to provide the desired result. Having the facts, the manager can act. Having acted, the results can be weighed and further progress made.

Good organisation is growth resulting from the co-ordination of all the activities of a business. This is another way of saying that a manager must decide on objectives in all departments of a business so that everything works to the desired end. This entails:

(1) Full use of capital. No waste. All capital employed to bring about the final objective of the business.

(2) The making of profit.

(3) Full and effective use of labour.

(4) Best use of materials.

(5) Business growth.

(6) Promotion of good labour relations bringing about a happy workforce.

(7) Achievement of the largest possible sales.

(8) Reliable credit control.

The successful manager has to co-ordinate all these different aspects of running a business until the objectives of that business are achieved.

In building a new business the manager can fail through not being decisive in all important matters. With a full knowledge of the options the manager must take decisions without hesitation. The manager may fail through being over critical instead of constructive. The manager must not be impetuous and act on too little thought or information. Yet, at the same time, the manager should not vacillate when a solution or course of action is obvious.

A manager must learn to recognise what is a little problem and what is more important. There should be a desire to consult others and to use their knowledge and abilities. As far as possible, emergencies should be avoided, and this can be done with foresight based on a thorough knowledge of all the options. Cause and effect applies in business as much as in nature. Everything that happens has a cause. Everything a manager achieves is because certain actions were taken based on a full knowledge of the possibilities.

Managers make policies. Policy is the establishing of desired objectives through general principles that are laid down for operating the business. Policy guides action in:

- Sales

- Type of customer sought

- Best channels of distribution

- Fixing of prices

- Advertising and promotion

- Purchasing

- Production
- Credit terms
- Borrowing limits
- Staff relations.

A realisation of objectives will:

- Lay down standards of performance
- Aid the total direction of the business
- Promote sensible managerial control
- Make unproductive effort less likely.

We have already given thought to control of stock levels. It is worth repeating that buyers must ensure the right level of stock is available when needed. A business should be able to fulfil its orders promptly. I thoroughly detest and mistrust television and press advertising that calls for 28 days to fulfil an order. Why should the public, that is the buyer, finance these traders? Why should they hold the money so long before parting with the goods?

- Good management ensures prompt fulfilling of orders.

A basic consideration in regard to the starting of a business depends on the amount of liability a person wishes to assume. If self employed, and therefore your own boss, you can have complete freedom of action. Nobody to please but yourself. A sole proprietorship is the easiest way to set up a business, as we have seen in Chapter 1, and it also has the advantage that, because no-one else has to be considered, prompt action is more certain. Complete secrecy is also possible and the business is usually economical to run.

There is great pleasure and a sense of fulfilment from running your own business. Success brings considerable kudos. The main argument against sole ownership is the fact that a sole owner is fully liable for all the commitments of the business. It is likely that the owner's home is used as security for a loan or overdraft but, this does mean it is fairly easy to obtain credit because suppliers know that they can claim against all the businessman's assets if things go wrong. If the business is a success then all the profits are yours. If it is a failure the result can be heartbreaking.

In Chapter 1 we considered some of the disadvantages of a partnership but this can be a way forward if you do not wish to work alone with total responsibility for everything. With both partners providing capital, the business can be financed more adequately than would be the case with just one owner, and the profits can be shared in whatever proportion is deemed appropriate. We have already said that two heads are better than one. Each partner can fill the role he or she is most suited to. Each can specialise in what they do best.

- It is vital that a partner is chosen carefully as an unhappy partnership in business is unlikely to be successful.

It is perhaps an advantage if one is a super sales person and the other an excellent manager, organiser or financial expert. In a partnership liability is shared, and jointly all the partners are liable for all the debts of the business, just as the one person is so liable in sole ownership. It remains just as possible in a partnership to lose everything. This is the main disadvantage. It is possible that what started out as a great meeting of minds may not continue as such. It is not always possible to maintain harmony. An error made by one partner can ruin both. Also, a partnership is hard to sell.

The least risky way of entering business is to form a limited company in which the liability of each director is limited. In addition to this main advantage a limited company is an entity in itself. Directors can join or leave and the company continues. After some years, if the company has been built up successfully, a shareholding director can sell the shares and retire. If the company fails the directors are not liable beyond their original share commitment and any guarantees they have made.

Forgetting for the moment the thought of precautions against losses, no doubt the sole ownership business is likely to be the most fun and the most satisfying. However, all beginners in business should know that more than a quarter of new businesses fail.

- It cannot be emphasised too strongly that business is all about taking risks.

No-one should be afraid to enter business because of the risk, but all should be aware of the risk. The risk to be taken is not a reason to stay away from the adventure. The enterprising take risks and many make fortunes. It is always possible to be successful despite the risk. It is just as possible to make a profit as to make a loss. However, many do not make a profit or earn only the same or less than many employed persons. It is not really worthwhile accepting all the risks of being self employed to earn less than a labourer. It is therefore important to learn how to run a business with some prospect of success.

Most businesses do not make a profit. Remember this, and study to be a success. To own a business gives you the chance of self expression and achievement. Learn to do what you do really well. In your business, aim to give a good service to your customers and clients. Build a business in which others will want to work. Use your personality to obtain the credit to expand. Learn about and like people. Study to get along with people. People are your business.

Deal in facts. Be scientific in the conduct of your business and in the way you deal with customers, suppliers and employees. Make people want to deal with you. Other things being equal a buyer will place orders with the supplier he or she likes best. Getting to be liked is a two-edged sword with which to win your battles. If your customers and staff like you, you are on your way.

- The customers must like you. They must also like what you offer – make or sell what the customer wants.

Site your business well. If in manufacturing, be close to the source of materials, if you can, and certainly be close to good staff. If in wholesale, have good parking space for your trade customers. If in retail, then be on the best side of the road, on a corner, close to the big stores, remembering that position can be all important.

Because of the great number of business failures it has to be said that prospects are not good. However, in such circumstances many rise and become successful. You must have sound policies. You must build a good organisation. You must use your time to the best advantage. Train staff to be able to undertake the successful promotion of the objectives of the business. A good businessman will encourage expressions of ability by members of staff. One of the most essential aspects of management is the ability to bring the best out of others. You must make others want to please you with outstanding work. If you do not deserve loyalty you will not get it. If you do not enthuse with the people who work for you, their results will be mediocre.

Enthusiasm is catching. I often go round booksellers

promoting my books and, to my surprise, a bookseller once said to me, 'I marvel at your enthusiasm.' I was much complimented by this statement but said to the bookseller, 'How can I expect you to care about my books if I don't?' Another bookseller wrote to me: 'It was refreshing to meet someone as enthusiastic and cheerful in the book trade as yourself.' I was delighted to receive this testimony. I do wonder how the other publishers and their representatives behave when calling on this bookseller.

If you want to succeed in selling goods to customers, you must be enthusiastic. Remember to laugh and have the world laughing with you. If you cry, you will probably be left to cry alone.

Your staff want to believe in what they are doing. Nothing is so soul destroying as, day after day, doing things in which you have no compelling interest. If you are going to work just to earn a living it is more than likely that your staff will do the same. You will be surrounded by miserable people longing for the end of the day's work. Also, the customers to whom you hope to sell your products will probably be as lethargic as you are. Wake up, and put your whole self into what you do.

- Enjoy what you do. Show the enthusiasm you feel for your business and your product, and others will tend to believe what you say.

To return to the more mundane matter of money – you must have money to survive. This should come in from sales made with reasonable credit control, and from investments or loans. Here, again, if you want the bank to believe in your business, it is important that you should believe in yourself and what you are doing and what you want to do. Why should anyone lend money to an unenthusiastic and pessimistic would-be borrower? I wouldn't! You must have money, so present yourself as worthy of orders, loyalty and trust.

A manager should always be aware of the state of the business, aware of whether the turnover is going up or down. A manager must know about any influences that will have a bearing on the business. These influences include government action, the attitude of banks, the outlook of customers, the outlook of the sales people. Every aspect of a business must be constantly under review. New ideas and new methods of production, packaging and marketing must be produced when there is any slowing down of trade.

- You do not have to fail.

3

SELLING A BUSINESS

Following on from the last chapter we must consider the possibility that one day you might want to sell the business. There is much to think about in relation to such a sale. Do you want to sell the whole business outright or only an interest while retaining some interest for yourself?

If your business has not worked out as well as you expected it may be possible to achieve the original expectations by selling all or part of the business thus bringing into it both additional abilities and additional working capital. All the business needs for success may be renewed energy, a sharper mind, better sales and more capital.

If the business has been as great a success as you planned, your reason for selling might be that you want to retire and have time to enjoy the fruits of your success.

You can sell for one immediate payment or you can sell in a way that brings in income over a number of years. It may be easier to find a purchaser who would wish to spread the purchase payment over a period.

Remember taxation rules are complex and you will want to take advice from your accountant on the most tax efficient way of disposing of the business.

4

IMPROVING A BUSINESS

In most situations in life there is room for improvement. If attention is constantly given to the improvement of a business it is doubtful if it will ever be in trouble. It is vital to keep up-to-date with methods of production and modern sales methods. A business must move with the times or die. Progress will defeat deterioration. A constant check should be kept on all aspects of the business.

Sales are the life blood of any business and sales methods must be constantly monitored. As well as in sales, it is important to introduce modern techniques in all areas of the business. The useless members of an organisation must always be rooted out.

Financial policy may need to be changed; for example, with more emphasis on selling for cash than for credit. Alternatively, the correct action might be to allow extended credit to encourage more spending. To obtain more working capital it might pay to offer a settlement discount on your invoices to bring the money in more quickly.

To keep a business profitable it may be necessary to discontinue old lines that no longer command the support they once did. This will enable all the capital to be concentrated behind the best sellers in the business. A cut in staff numbers may be necessary to reduce costs and thus increase profitability.

There are many ways of marketing goods. It will pay to find the best method for your business. You might employ a sales organisation exclusively instead of appointing your own sales team. You might sell direct to the public rather than through trade channels. Whatever you decide, back it up with sound and often repeated advertising.

Sometimes it is possible to suggest new uses for a product. Also, new customers can be attracted by offering larger discounts or by taking smaller orders, or by allowing longer credit. Business can often be boosted by agreeing to accept the return of unsold goods or by agreeing to pay for local advertising. Improvements can be made in packaging to make the product more attractive.

Improvements can result from increasing efficiency. This can be achieved by cutting out overlapping functions or by making sure that there is a regular check on the effectiveness of all efforts. Do they still achieve the aim originally intended or could they benefit from change?

- Keep all effort under constant review and encourage regular discussion of options.

Make sure that revision of methods does follow discussion that calls for changes to be made. Remember that stagnation is death, whereas revision and adaptation can lead to improved results.

Give very defined responsibility for different functions. Leave nothing to chance. Employ specialists in all departments. There is no substitute for the best. Keep records that allow future planning and control without problems. Design matters so that all wasteful effort shows up and can be eliminated. Encourage attractive sales and advertising programmes. Make your staff happy and secure so that they all value their employment. Encourage initiative in every employee. Ensure that all possible suggestions will receive executive attention and consideration.

Do not allow your staff to feel left out of planning for future success. Act promptly on all good suggestions so that nobody feels unimportant. Make special rewards for ideas that improve business efficiency and increase turnover. Work for the friendliest possible relationship between all staff and top executives.

Interest should be shown in all the efforts of staff. No member of staff should be made to feel inferior and without worth. In your locality be known as a good employer. The Japanese manage this in a masterly way. They manage to involve employees in accepting responsibilities as well as benefits and improvements in staff conditions. Achieve this as far as is possible. See that all levels of staff meet and discuss the operation of the business and its policy for the future. Seek to promote your own staff whenever possible, rather than bring in experienced people from outside the business.

- Make consultation, not dictation, the hallmark of employee relations.

Take the trouble to explain why unpopular decisions have been made for the long-term good of the business. Make the working conditions comfortably the best possible, remembering that contented staff will produce more for the business than a bank loan. Be sure that staff understand that extravagant claims for higher wages can only harm the business and ultimately themselves. Aim at authority without injustice.

5

CONTROLLING A BUSINESS

The business with the most inefficient management is most at risk from fraud and petty pilfering. If any wastage is allowed, for example of stationery, it signals the impression that stock will not be missed. Very low wages may contribute to an atmosphere where pilfering is rife.

When engaging staff make a thorough check by obtaining character references and if the references are not good, do not take a chance by employing someone dubious.

The most likely fraud arises from slackness in checking expense accounts. Pay a good salary and be strict on what expenses can be claimed.

- A small fiddle can lead to more serious fraud. Kill the outbreak of a fire at its source and the building will not burn down.

Fraud must not be allowed because it cuts away at the profit level the business needs to stay viable. The closer the business is to break even the more life threatening fraud becomes and even the tiniest pilfering has to be stopped.

Fraud can be avoided to a large extent simply by having a system of checking by one member of staff on another. For example, one member of staff might place the order but another one would be responsible for checking in the goods. One person records the sale and someone else charges the customer's account and yet another banks the money. The person who approves a purchase does not also issue the payment.

It is often the case that an irregularity will show up when a staff member is on holiday or is ill and someone else has to cover their position. Encourage staff to take their holiday entitlement and be suspicious of anyone in a position of trust who does not. You should also try and discover the financial health of your staff and avoid putting temptation in the way of anyone you know to be in need of financial help. It is better to provide the help they need than to risk being robbed!

Most large fraud involves cheques so ensure that bank statements are reconciled properly by someone senior who is not involved in the signing or banking of cheques. If possible, make it necessary to have two signatures on cheques especially those for large amounts.

While there can be fraud involving cheques, the most likely fraud will involve the handling of cash. For this reason, it is vital to have precise records of all cash transactions.

- Managers responsible for cash and for signing cheques should not make fraud easy.

Use modern equipment as much as possible. Give, and obtain, authorised receipts for all transactions. Cash coming into the business should not be used for paying for supplies, which should be paid for out of a separate fund.

Make someone responsible for issuing postage stamps or monitoring the use of the franking machine.

- Take out insurance against the risks of fraudulent losses.

If possible bank every day. Receipts must be given for all payments received by sales or other staff. Impress upon customers that they must get a receipt for any cash paid. This must be an official receipt on company stationery.

Earlier I mentioned the importance of controlling expense accounts. Make it clearly understood that payment will only be made for verifiable expenses. Compare expense accounts, especially where, for example, someone new is taking over an existing job.

- Keep a record of expenses as a percentage of turnover.

If you employ someone to sell and the percentage is higher than you would pay a self-employed agent then your sales person is not doing a good enough job and should be replaced.

You could pay a bonus to the sales person whose expenses are the lowest in relation to sales. Also you should pay expense accounts promptly.

Budgeting will help to improve the performance of a business. The objective of budgeting is to obtain the best possible turnover from the least possible cost. Good budgeting reduces costs by identifying potential waste that can be eliminated. Money will only be made available for projects that have been decided on in advance.

- Encouraging each department to work out a sensible budget fixes responsibility on the managers preparing the budget.

Overtrading should not happen because the business will be run on the basis of well authenticated facts rather than on over enthusiastic optimism.

- Budgets should cover only periods for which you have the ability to accurately forecast cost and revenue.

To make a workable and reliable budget, first determine exactly what total money will be available. If what you want to achieve cannot be managed within the budget you must cut down your programme until its cost balances with the money available.

The sales budget is the most important because without sales there will not be funds for anything else. The production budget can be fitted to the expected sales. It is essential that overproduction is avoided and stocks must be kept in line with expected sales.

The final test of a manager's efficiency is seen in the performance of the business. There is a considerable difference between the results achieved by an average manager and those of a really good manager. The better manager shows a mastery of economic performance and no money is wasted.

A business manager has a wide range of responsibilities including managing other managers. There is the responsibility for training. There is the skill of knowing when and what to delegate. There is the constant appreciation of the need to generate profits. There is the responsibility for guiding the business to produce goods which meet a widely felt need among the population.

- Profits are made by meeting needs.

It is a fallacy to think that any businessman can be trained to be a good manager. It has been said that if any businessman can be a good manager then all art students can become Rembrandts.

- The good manager has to be dedicated to the job.

The job demands a complete and sound knowledge of every aspect of the business. The good manager must have the mental ability to consider problems and to make the decisions which solve the problems. And, it is important to grasp the nub of the situation and not spend time correcting lesser problems.

- The good manager gets things done.

There is the ability to inspire others and to gain their loyalty. Judgements must be mature and not half-baked. All thinking must be sound and not shallow.

- A good manager will not make many mistakes.

A hallmark is learning from and not repeating mistakes. There will be an appreciation of the mistakes made by others in the past and a quickness to grasp the facts relating to present problems. Nothing will be accepted as gospel. The good manager will be creative, forming original ideas and objectives.

A top manager is of necessity a person of integrity. Interest in people will be sustained. As a result staff will like their manager and will like to please him or her. This manager knows that people matter.

There will be a consistency and persistency in working to fulfil objectives. In riding the difficulties the manager will remember that there is no excellence if there are no difficulties. Policy decisions will be backed up by observation and intelligent initiative.

Some managers who do not reach the top level are overkeen on discipline and tend to smother initiative in others. This kind of management ignores the flair that can bring success by innovation. This is a mistake. To succeed, the manager must not be slow on the uptake or appear ambiguous. A manager can fail through lack of decisiveness or by impetuous action.

- The overriding purpose of a business is to find and keep customers. The business exists because the customer exists.

If there are no customers there is no business. If the number of customers does not increase or the amount of business from existing customers does not grow, then the business can stagnate and die. If the business does not make customers then it does not make anything worthwhile. Without customers there can be no profit. Without profit there is no point to the business.

- The most important person to a business is its customer.

It follows that the customer must be the most important person to the business manager. That is why the manager must study to improve marketing techniques, because marketing is often the whole business from the customer's point of view. The customer does not see the discussions, the board meetings, the staff appraisals – only the marketing in its final form. It is therefore important that a business, in addition to providing goods, must endeavour to make more economical, appealing and improved goods. Everything a manager does must be aimed at satisfying customers. Everything should be looked at from the customer's point of view.

A business manager has to decide who the customers are. Are they traders or the general public? Once it is decided who the customers are, then every endeavour must be made to appeal to and satisfy the customers.

Having decided who the market is, the manager must work out the size of the market to be catered for. How large a part can the business reasonably expect to reach. It is no good producing 10,000 items for a market that needs only 1,000. On the other hand it would be a pity to make only 20 to meet a call for 500!

In the publishing business, for example, if you were going to publish a book on salesmanship you would first find out how many sales people there are and how many people in the next year might want to learn to sell. Then you would consider how many of those could you reasonably expect to reach.

One way of pleasing customers is to think of new products or ways of improving existing products. The good manager must be able to innovate in the interests of good customer relations. Innovation can apply to sales methods as well as to production.

- No business can live forever on past achievements.

Innovation will keep customers interested. An interested customer buys the goods on offer and the business makes profits. Profits are the ultimate test of business efficiency. Profits provide the finance for future operations.

Management must decide which objectives are the most important in the business. Objectives include such aims as higher unit sales, bigger profits, improved production output, new sources of profit, etc.

Management must decide on priorities in the interests of the customer. Maintaining the right balance is the hallmark of good management. A good manager will rightly predict trends.

- It is the job of management to do today what will lead to better business tomorrow.

Management must control costs. A good manager will seek

to know what is being done that is not necessary, will cut it out and reduce costs. Management must realise the company's objectives.

Management will achieve good staff relationships by ensuring that special effort or achievement is well rewarded. The manager must, in all this, find job satisfaction and set for himself or herself high standards of workmanship. Doers are leaders.

A manager must set the objectives and organise so that the objectives are achieved. This requires skill in motivating others to achieve their best performance all the time and, to succeed, the manager must be a good communicator.

A manager successfully directing events will prevent emergencies from arising. This will require self confidence, mental agility, administrative skills, ambition and application to achieve success.

If it is agreed that the person who matters is the customer, then the manager must get the most possible out of the staff. To this end all treatment of staff has to be seen to be fair. In order to cultivate motivation, the human needs of staff have to be considered.

Staff need to be assured of job preservation. As human beings they feel the need to belong, to be accepted and to be valued.

All workers need to preserve self esteem and status. All must be given the opportunity for self fulfilment. They must be encouraged to realise their full potential.

- Management must be sure that wages are fair. Security is valued.

Workers' rights must be respected. Management should provide a procedure for dealing with grievances. Working conditions must constantly improve with improvements in the profitability of the business so the workers can feel they share in the success.

- Workers must have status according to ability. Job titles are important. Privileges should come with promotion.

Management should be aware that incentives should not only be in the provision of more money but should include praise and commendation for good ideas and work well done.

In order to be able to do all the good things which make for good staff relations and also to be innovative in production and distribution, finance is vital.

- The realisation of competitiveness may well depend on a satisfactory financial position.

At the start of a business, and before making improvements, there is the need for initial finance. There must be sufficient capital to uphold the business until income exceeds outlay. This finance will continue to be needed not just until the goods are sold but until the monies from the sales are received.

- There is often a considerable difference in time between making the sale and being paid for it.

Initial finance must fill the gap. Management must make sure that the operations of the business will justify the investment.

Management must have a full knowledge of not just production costs but the costs of making the sale, and income must be estimated realistically.

At first, cash must be preserved carefully. This means seeking extended credit terms, buying in small quantities, limiting advertising, having a skeleton staff. Management has to work out how long it will take for sales to reach the point where some of these restrictions can be lifted.

The business needs to have available enough money to run the business until conversion of money into goods and back again into money is fast enough to meet all the commitments of the business.

- To have sufficient working capital is a must or you may lose the business.

Having the working capital, the business must make more than the cost of the money plus enough to cover all outgoings. It is important to decide how far it is safe to go into debt. Take advantage of trade credit and borrow against receivables.

It must be remembered that capital alone will not make a good business. Many people have started a business with all the capital they could ever need, yet they have not succeeded.

- Given the capital, the businessman must build an organisation.

It is organisation that multiplies a one-man business into a large corporation. There are limitations to what one person can do, and the difference between a small and a large company is mainly organisation. If a well organised business is founded, the owner can be free to use his or her skills to the full. A good organisation will eliminate waste and increase opportunity.

The most thorough organisation is necessary in several aspects of a business. We have already seen that it is essential for organisation to link finance and accounting, production, sales and marketing and distribution.

- For a business to reach the heights of success it needs solid organisation in planning, operation and control.

In planning most factors are related to the overwhelmingly important forecast of sales revenue. Sales are always of major importance in any business. Organisation will provide checks as required and costs must be reduced if sales fall.

We have already considered the importance of the customer who, above all else, wants deliveries on time, regular calls from the sales person, accurate accounts, reliable products and a prompt response to complaints. In considering the needs of customers, management must also insist that customers pay promptly for their supplies.

Your sales team should be providing regular information on the creditworthiness of customers. You should add to this, information gleaned from trade and bank references and from credit agencies.

Be willing to exchange credit information with other companies as you may well be glad to receive information from them on occasions. This sort of information is usually very reliable and up-to-date. The amount of credit you give should not be determined by the sales person who may be more concerned with turnover than creditworthiness. You can be generous with new customers as you will find that they may be loyal to you for many years.

If you think a customer is in some difficulty, first of all see how you can help, for your assistance during a cash-flow crisis will, again, reward you with customer loyalty.

Make sure you are not supplying to figure heads for people who are bad credit risks. Get to know the people who will pay the bills.

- Good credit control will help to protect the money you have earned.

No business can stand still. It should be expected that a good business, well managed, will grow by approximately 20 per cent each year. With this in mind management should forecast likely sales, compare with the competition, improve packaging and publicity, achieve the sales targets in all areas and maintain good customer relations.

The risks that can hold back a business and counter any possibility of growth are:

1 Incompetent management
2 Inexperienced management
3 Shortage of working capital
4 Superior competition
5 Overtrading
6 Underselling
7 Extravagance.

Call them the seven deadly sins and avoid them.

The management with the most ingenuity, keenness and foresight will survive. What is needed is thorough knowledge, skill, experience and aggression. These qualities should lead to increased sales and reduced costs.

A business will improve with good incentives to staff, by purchasing goods at more favourable prices, by cutting out waste and all unnecessary procedures, by improved sales, by cutting out unprofitable lines, and by finding new markets. In retail businesses, improvements will come from better display of goods, better and more friendly service, incentives to staff, better lighting and more space.

All that has been said means that a business needs good customer relations and good employee relations. For good customer relations your company must appear to be good. Managers must be good judges of timeliness, of suitability of the product, of good taste in the product, and of presentation. Why should people buy your product? Why have they stopped buying your product?

Treat customers as friends. Find out what people like and offer it. Minimise complaints. Offer good sales aids. Stop ill-will from growing. Cut the causes of complaints. Keep promises.

Do not supply substitutes without permission. Answer all letters promptly. An individual letter from the boss to a customer is worth many sales. Congratulate good customers. Thank prompt payers.

Retailers serve the final customer and their shop should be attractive and light, offering easy access, and there should be an atmosphere of friendly interest in the customer. Be absolutely honest always. Be courteous and pleasant. Be patient. Put customers at ease. Do as you say you will do. Remember that public relations are all about attitude.

Good staff relations will produce good customer relations. Never publicly reprimand a member of staff. Let your staff be proud. Show an interest in your staff. Satisfied employees are an invaluable asset. Consider that pride in one's work results in good work. Each employee will appreciate the personal interest taken in him or her.

Security means good morale. Each member of staff will appreciate fair treatment, and being listened to. He or she will like to feel their work is appreciated, will want to know a lot about the company and will be grateful for explanations on why certain things are being done. All will be glad of the opportunity for promotion within the company, and will feel proud that their company is well thought of in the locality.

- A proud and satisfied employee is the best advertisement a company can have.

Finally, in this chapter I want to say a little more about control of costs. Controlled cost is another expression for efficiency. Uncontrolled cost is like a deadly poison and will kill the business eventually.

When deciding on objectives, management must at the same time consider the cost of attaining the objective. Making a decision about which objectives can be afforded is a key part of managerial control. One crucial aim, as we have said, is the elimination of all waste and to strive for value for money. Compare effort and accomplishment.

- To achieve low costs it is necessary to compare estimates with actual costs.

If there is a difference, find out why and if it could have been avoided, or if there was a mistake in the estimate. It is important that the selling price of the product should be enough to cover all costs and to show a profit.

- You cannot plan for profits without planning for costs.

Managers must work out the break-even point and if it is possible to attain this. It must be worked out what increase in sales is necessary to justify a lower selling price. What happens to the profit when there is a change in price? When considering advertising, work out how much can be spent to obtain increased sales? Work out how much it costs to fulfil orders.

The general expenses of running the business (overheads), and the cost of making and fulfilling the sale, must be added to the cost price when calculating the correct selling price.

Management budgets should establish objectives and measure performance. Budgets will tell the business manager when more capital is needed to attain objectives. Thoroughly considered budgets will prevent waste of resources, and show the most economical use of resources and labour. If the results fall short of the desired objective, management must consider changes in strategy. For example, if costs are running too high it might be necessary to move from blanket to selective selling.

- The control that management must impose on a business should not be seen as red tape.

Unnecessary work of any kind must be avoided. Make sure that all reports serve a purpose and if they do, be certain they are produced regularly and distributed to the right people. Sales should be analysed by product and by territory.

Authority should be required for all orders placed by the company. All supplies and finished goods should be checked in and out. All prices charged in and out must be as directed. Stock levels must be kept to the amounts agreed.

- Simplify all paper work.

If forms are used they should be easy to use and the reason for them should be understood by all concerned. Forms must be controlled or they will occupy an unacceptable amount of staff and management time. Do what is necessary and do nothing that has no purpose.

- Good management will constantly reduce unit costs and increase overall profitability.

6

STAFF SELECTION

The main aim you must have in mind when selecting staff is to engage workers who are ideal for the positions you want to fill. You can follow a system of employment psychology that will find the most suitable people for your purpose and help you to make them happy in their positions and loyal to your company.

The aim of employment psychology in management is to provide incentives to use capacity to the limit. For consideration come methods of work, hours, rest times, elimination of wasteful activity, and reduction of fatigue. The overall aim is to achieve the greatest possible output per employee without increasing fatigue. This can be referred to as the psychology of efficiency.

Once you have selected the best men and women for your purpose and attained the optimum effort under the best possible conditions you can turn your attention to the sale of your product.

- It is important that you measure rather than guess the ability of applicants for employment.

You need to be assured that workers have the ability to perform the tasks to be undertaken. You will make some mistakes. You must get rid of the inefficient as soon as it becomes obvious that they are not right for the job.

Do not underestimate ability. Place everyone according to their ability. Do not waste talent. Someone who is in a position where they could be doing something much more taxing is being wasted just as much as if you were employing someone who is idle. Deal with misfits quickly, and readily promote those that show they have exceptional ability. It is contended that the ability to do many occupations is inborn rather than learned.

- Be careful not to place people in positions for which they are unsuited.

It is the nature of things that the majority of employees will prove to be of average ability. When considering applicants check for the amount of ability. A small man will not fit a large position.

Psychologists say that the strongest single environmental factor is education. However, it is a fact that education alone will not materially alter the nature of individuals. Mental ability is often inborn and does not arise from education. Many people have inborn capacities that will not be increased by education or environment.

A diseased plant will not benefit from being placed in better soil. Fundamental capacities are there to be used and little altered by training. The training will merely add the tool with which to work. It has been observed that children in the same family and brought up in the same environment grow to be less alike. Individual differences are increased and not inhibited by practice. The person who is originally better at doing something will improve faster than someone whose initial performance was not so good. Native abilities will not be altered by training, only directed. There is a difference between capacities and abilities. Ability or skill can be modified by environment when learning a trade or acquiring a habit. Skills are enhanced by training.

If after training the abilities of two trainees are compared it will become obvious that differences existed and were born into the individuals. These are capacities. After the same training one person will be better than the other because he or she has more aptitude or inborn capacity for the work in hand.

- Training does not alter capability. The brightest remains the brightest and the dullard remains dull.

The final skills attained by a person are the result of capacity plus training. Abilities cannot be increased in a person whose capabilities are low. Training can be provided for a certain purpose. Capacities have to be taken as they are. Good training is based on a realisation of the capacities that are evident. A cow dressed up as a man with a pipe in its mouth is still a cow! A worker with little capacity will only be a mediocre worker.

- Try and obtain information about an applicant's family background. This may well tell you more than any number of letters of recommendation.

Tests for applicants must be reliable. A good test will produce the same result from the same person a few weeks apart. If it does not, it is merely a puzzle. A real measure of ability is a measure that can measure correctly what it is supposed to measure. You cannot measure the temperature of boiling water with a slide rule.

- A company that has the right people in the right jobs will have a lower turnover of staff.

You cannot measure fitness for a job situation from a letter of application. The writing in a letter has no relevance to a person's fitness to do a particular job of work. All the letter shows is the legibility of the person's handwriting.

When choosing staff for your company be as thorough as you would be when ordering supplies. Remember that in an interview situation you can only gain a first impression. For many jobs, particularly those involving selling, this is not enough. Applicants will almost always overrate their ability and suitability for the job.

- When you make a selection from the applicants be convinced that you are taking on someone who is ideal, and not just the best from a bad bunch.

You need to know the history of an applicant but believe nothing without proof. Do not accept the applicant's opinion of him or her self. Consider several references from an applicant and check them out thoroughly.

Your aim is to find successful employees. Consider the traits you wish to find in your staff. Make a list and give marks for each trait as you interview and consider each applicant. Decide which are the most important traits and weight the marks accordingly. For example you might have an ideal age range. You may want to give marks for how well educated the candidate is and how experienced at the type of job. Perhaps it is important to you whether or not the person is married.

To determine desired traits compare the successes and failures known to you. Think about your experience of the best and worst workers.

A good test will increase your chances of having good staff, and with it increased profitability. Devise the test so that it requires little writing and make the questions specific. There should be many items but only one answer to each. The questions should be such that they bring out information about the abilities and capabilities of the candidate in relation to the job.

There are various ways of recruiting staff and it is possible that they will all be used at different times. In the previous chapter we considered the value of promotion from within, which tends to be popular and encourages loyalty. A considerable source of staff to any company, large or small, is to be found among the friends and relatives of existing employees. This again will help to build a friendly atmosphere and encourage the loyalty that is so important to a successful business. Staff can be found through the careers tutors at the local schools and colleges, through employment agencies (who charge a fee), by contacting the trades union and, of course, by advertising in your local paper.

7

ADVERTISING AND
PUBLIC RELATIONS

Advertising and public relations should be used to create goodwill. When you have new products you should write with information to appropriate newspapers, magazines and trade journals. Remember that half a column of editorial comment is worth far more than a page of advertising. Well produced adverts will bring results but it is independent editorial comment that will go further in promoting a good image of your company.

- Give somebody on your staff the responsibility of looking out for opportunities to promote the business and its products through free publicity.

Find out who at your local newspaper should be informed of any newsworthy item and do not overlook the value of publicity shots and comment backed up by advertising in trade papers.

Remember that, as far as the national press is concerned, news is only news for a day. Therefore you should not delay if you have something of general interest. Even the local weekly papers want their news items to be fresh.

Local newspapers are usually interested in such things as financial statements, expansion plans especially if it creates new jobs in the area, sporting success, directors' involvement in local activities outside the business, human interest and anniversaries.

Trade papers will be more interested in new products, senior appointments, expansion plans especially into new markets, changes in sales policy or personnel, public statements by directors, and they like to be supplied with interesting photographs.

- Become involved with trade associations.

- Treat all callers to your premises in such a way that they will be glad to return.

Work hard to project the right image to trade customers. Make them feel that their business, however small, is welcome. Potential customers will form an impression of your business and will feel that you are good to do business with. Use all correspondence as an opportunity to create immediate or future sales, or both.

- Everything you say or write should be doing a sales job for your company. Be appreciative of prompt payment and deal immediately with all queries and complaints.

Advertising is wasteful unless it succeeds in its objective of producing action. Good advertising will bring about a reaction that will lead to sales. Generally, people do not like advertisements and tend to ignore them. They therefore have to be made to look at and then read the advertisement if the money paid out by the businessman is not to be a waste. Sometimes the public can be surprised by an interesting advertisement and this is an indication of the success of the advertiser in getting the message across.

If possible advertising should reveal something new

about the product or some new use to which it can be put. Sometimes, though it is worth producing reminder adverts which should simply be a statement of the obvious.

- Good advertising will firstly be interesting. Having caught the attention of the reader, it should then inform and finally be an inducement to purchase.

You can learn much from studying advertisements and working out why they attract and compel attention. A good advertising campaign does not just happen. A great deal of thought lies behind any successful advertising series. There is a story behind most products and it is this story that should be told.

- You must train yourself to think interestingly if you are to convey interest to the public.

Some advertisements stand out from the general run of notices. It is the outstanding advert that captures the interest, is remembered and gets the response. Consistently good advertising creates a sense of confidence in the product that will lead to increased sales of that product and others from the same company.

An orator preparing a speech will make notes of all the salient points to be covered. These are written with the most important point as the climax of the speech. Just as much attention should be given to the preparation of an advertisement. The first sentence of a speech should demand attention and an advert needs to be just as arresting. If you do not grab attention you will not compel action.

Headlines should be short, as in these examples:

- Murphy TV . . . see for yourself.

- Temptation on Toast.

- Tyres with Teeth.

- Don't be vague . . . ask for Haig.

- You never have to shake a Watermans.

- We made signs before we could talk.

- Worth a guinea a box.

- It beats as it sweeps as it cleans.

There are many more. They strike home and the really good ones remain in the memory for years.

In trade adverts it is better to concentrate on getting over the facts. Sales points should be emphasised and it is best if illustrations are included.

Even in small spaces the use of white space is important. Adverts that look crammed and cluttered do not get attention. Illustration is almost always essential and type-faces need to be chosen carefully and professionally. Type must be clear and readable whatever its design.

- Your advert should emphasise the need or desire
  that is met by the product.

Make much of any exclusive feature. Say why the product should be bought. Think about who would want to buy the product and choose publications that those people would read. This is vital and you should think about age range, sex, living styles, town or country, etc.

Make it easy for prospective purchasers to buy your product. Advertise during the right seasons. You should not expect much response to an advert for bikinis if it is snowing outside.

- Make a point of highlighting any savings in cost over
  competing products.

Appeal to people's sense of greed, vanity, hunger, fear, love, etc. All advertising copy should be written with the thought that the objective is to sell. Be sincere. Be believable. Make your claim. Offer a definite benefit. Provoke immediate action.

Advertising of highly fashionable products should be appealing to a sense of prestige and authority. Keep the copy brief. Do not bother with details. Make the potential customer believe that they are in fact influencing fashion.

An advertising campaign should automatically arise from the market situation once it is understood. It is well worth noting that the aim is to offer people not what we think they want but what they actually do want! But, people do not always know what they want until they are shown it, so to that extent the job of the advert is to inform. Before the invention of the wheel, when everyone walked, no-one gave a thought to needing transport. Advertising should lead to betterment. Advertising should inform.

In preparing advertising campaigns consider that you should be appealing to desires or, if applicable, you should be creating desires for something that will affect and improve the life style of a great many people.

Generally, advertising should appeal to one or more of the following:

□ Pride in appearance

□ Security

□ Pleasure

□ Recreation

□ Proficiency

□ Economy

- Distinctiveness
- Ability
- Cleanliness
- Health
- Taste
- Ambition
- Giving
- Childcare
- Property
- Savings
- Provision for old age
- Time saving
- Freedom from drudgery
- Entertainment
- Durability
- Home comforts
- Food enjoyment
- Romance
- Sexual prowess.

Specialised advertising to trade customers should appeal to:

- Insurance against loss
- Economy in use
- Repairs and service

- Longevity in use (especially machinery)
- Productivity
- Dependability
- Quality
- Simplicity
- Sales aids
- Punctuality.

While advertising informs it must always go further and sell the goods. Advertising is a waste of money if it fails to sell.

- Advertising must meet standards of honesty and decency.

Most promotion of goods by businessmen is honest, perhaps more so than in the promotion of religion or politics! This is because it is vital for advertisements to be factual. There is nothing evil in the promotion or creation of desire.

There are good reasons why people should desire to improve their lot in life, should desire to be loving and romantic, should want to maintain good health and to pursue happiness. There is nothing wrong with persuasion that leads to improvement of the many facets of modern living and in turn to a stronger urge to work in order to achieve one's desires.

- Wealth is important to the success of advertising.

Where there is even a small amount of money not spoken for, the advertiser is competing with other advertisers for that money, for the little extra cash to be spent on their product. It is true that advertising first encourages regular spending and then uses persuasion to grab the extra money that might be available. In a free enterprise culture, competition is the very breath of life. Without advertising who would know what to buy? Who would be able to compare and thereby encourage better workmanship? Good managers enjoy the fight to achieve the best sales for their company. Growth to greater achievements, being pushed higher and higher, is the delight of the manager of a private enterprise.

- It is a thrill to put your business on top of its field.

This battle to be the best is good for all. Advertising to attain the top position benefits the customer. Advertising is good for all.

Advertising is news.
Advertising increases choice.
Advertising brings prices down.
Advertising improves quality.

- Good managers make good use of advertising and all other publicity opportunities.

There are people who feel that advertising is a cost that increases the price of a product but it can be argued that this is not the case. Successful advertising leads to increased sales that lead to longer production runs which usually leads to a lower unit cost. Competition spurred by advertising leads to selling at a competitive price in order to achieve best results. Managers must understand and believe this, and have a strategy that makes good use of advertising in all appropriate forms.

- Consistent advertising is the best insurance against a slump.

Management must realise that repetition is the hallmark of a successful advertising campaign. If it is worth saying, it is worth repeating.

Advertising must be a central instrument of company policy. Repetition must be regarded as one of the most important features of a campaign.

The psychology of advertising concerns itself with the public reaction to what it sees, feels, tastes, etc. What is it that attracts someone to what he or she sees? Advertising copy should be the application of psychology to the marketplace. You must grasp the principles involved in getting attention and compelling interest in order to write the best copy for your advertisements.

Advertising must be pleasing to the eye, arouse interest, and stimulate demand. The advertisement must make the prospect take action to buy. It has to show that the item will be of real benefit to the purchaser.

- Management must realise that people do want more, and better, goods to enhance their life style.

Every business manager must realise that in advertising there is a weapon to influence the trade to buy more of the company's products. Advertising helps the retailer. Good, truthful advertising builds up confidence in both the trade and the public.

Advertising is worthwhile because it brings new goods to the attention of the public much earlier than would otherwise be the case. Without advertising many items would cost more. Without advertising there would be less knowledge because advertising informs.

- Advertising must be planned to appear at the right time. It must coincide with the ability to supply the goods advertised.

It is important to have a name for the item so that it can be advertised repeatedly until thought of the product becomes synonymous with thought of the name. People still call their vacuum cleaner the "Hoover" whether it is or not.

- To support the advertising campaign there should be back-up material such as show cards that carry on the theme of the advertisements.

What every manager should seek is a good reputation for the company and its products. This grows naturally out of sound principles and quality control.

8

MARKETING AND SALES

It is worth repeating the thought that if you do not sell your goods you do not have a business. A concern without sales is a dead concern, like a pub without beer. Making the packaging attractive is a waste of money if no-one wants the product and it does not sell. You must sell what you make or die. The sales side of a business is its life blood. You must sell.

Let us study the marketing of a product. To market a product is to secure the highest profit by adding the maximum value at the minimum cost. Marketing also means finding out what the market thinks before producing the product, so that it is produced to meet a need.

To be successful in marketing you have to get to know your market. You should talk to people who are experts in the market you are entering. Take their advice on how the product is made. Manufacturing convenience must not be the first consideration. The product must eventually appear in packaging and at a price that will make it attractive to the potential buyer.

- An attractive deal must be offered.

Planning is also part of the marketing operation. A realistic sales target is worked out and sales aids prepared which will be included in offers to dealers. It is then up to the sales manager to organise the physical sales effort.

A sales forecast is made taking into account company policy on discounts and pricing. An advertising budget is worked out. The sales manager ensures that the sales people in the team are of the right calibre and in sufficient numbers to achieve the sales targets.

It should be borne in mind that no matter how much positive influence is brought to bear by good management, the level of sales will also be affected by matters outside the control of the company. For example, you cannot be expected to know for sure how your competitors will respond and government policy on taxation can change the nature of a market. It is possible to estimate changes in population and you should keep abreast of economic forecasts. Even world events can have an influence on trends and, of course, fashion is fickle.

- To anticipate, and be ready for, changes ahead of your competitors is the acme of good business management.

The marketing manager has to think through all the stages from the initial concept, to production of the item, how it will be packaged, advertised and distributed. A decision has to be made whether to sell through wholesale outlets, through the retail trade or direct to the public.

One problem of selling only through wholesalers is that they are carrying competitors' lines as well as your own. You cannot tell if your lines are being pushed hard or neglected. If you decide to sell through retailers it means much more work, but also more profit and greater control over marketing.

Some of the skill in marketing is in seeing the snags, as well as the advantages, and choosing a course of direction that will give the very best results for the business. The manager must obtain information and make things happen if the business is to succeed.

- There are trends in business that have to be watched.

For example, in cities there are now large shopping centres, where rents are high, and this means that the large stores dominate. Small shopkeepers can no longer afford the rents being asked. Their hopes lie in operating away from the city centres. In some industries there is a trend towards working from home where costs are very low.

- Nothing worthwhile will be achieved without knowledge.

Management must collect up-to-date information on products. Facts are the main weapon of the marketing manager. Keeping the facts up-to-date is a constant task as also is the review of costs. Is it possible to change to a more modern material that will also save money in production?

Packaging is no longer thought of as simply protection for a product. It has become very much a part of the advertising campaign. It is essential to monitor how the packaging is viewed by the market, and if the product itself does not need to change that does not mean that change is not needed in the packaging.

To feel confident that the company is operating at fullest efficiency, the business manager must monitor the following information:

- The size of the sales force.
- The number of calls made.

- The number of wholesalers covered and at what profit.

- The number of retailers covered and at what profit.

- The number of annual calls made on each.

- The average order from each.

The following questions need to be answered:

- Are the right competitive terms being offered to all traders?

- Is delivery as good as it should be?

- Are sufficient point-of-sale aids being supplied and used?

- Is credit control working properly?

The sales effort should be directed to achieve the stocking of the company's products in all possible outlets. However, unprofitable outlets should have their account closed and efforts redirected to the more profitable accounts. It is also worth considering closing accounts that are slow paying and increase efforts on those that pay quickly.

- Money coming into the business quickly lowers the cost of financing the operation and so increases profits.

It is much easier to make than to sell. Often very good ideas fail because not enough attention is given to salesmanship. Deliberate concentration must be applied to marketing and sales efforts or the best ideas, well produced and attractively packaged, will fail to earn profits. Most importantly, the concentration of sales effort should be directed to the right consumers.

- Do not aim at a void. Identify your customers and concentrate the effort towards them.

- Aim at the right age group.
- Aim at the right sex.

In all publicity and sales efforts avoid spending time and money chasing the wrong prospects. You will not sell many hearing aids to the young; some, but not many. Senior citizens do not buy many pop records! Aim right.

Keep in mind that times and conditions change. Do not overlook these changes or you may find that you have been addressing your efforts to the wrong areas and to the wrong people.

Make it easy for the retailer to sell your products. Good, well-directed advertising coupled with smart point-of-sale display will help considerably. This must be backed by good sales people who can be relied on for help and advice.

You can force the retailer to stock your lines by thorough advertising. Do not, however, advertise goods you cannot supply. We have already considered this to be a waste of time and money, but it is also extremely annoying to the retailer and to the retailer's customer.

The aim must be to get sufficient stock into *all* the outlets. What foolishness to create demand through advertising and then have the customer buy a competitor's product because yours has not arrived!

- There must be good stocks in all areas covered by advertising.

A good relationship with all customers is vital. Misunderstandings create enemies. Always help the retailer in every way possible. A marketing manager should visit some of the places he or she expects to sell in, starting with the main centres of population. It may be found that a few retailers are doing most of the business for you. Concentrate on helping these retailers.

- One day a month spent on the territory with the sales person can be very informative and it provides the opportunity to make friends with the retailers.

Point-of-sale material must be used in the shops and stores. Checks must be made that other products are not being displayed in your material. Do not underestimate the value of point-of-sale material because a very great deal is bought on impulse. Every piece of display material should make your company better known. Make different display material for different outlets. Some retailers want floor displays but others prefer to have it on the counter or on the walls. Make sure that what you supply is being used; it cannot sell for you if it is left in the storeroom.

- To judge if display material is effective compare sales before and after it has been installed.

It is obviously important that what you do succeeds in its purpose. Advertising must be in the correct medium and must tie in with other sales efforts. Advertising without adequate distribution is a marketing crime. And, of course, the product must be good.

- Remember that the only reason for a retailer to stock your product is because he or she expects to sell it.

Thinking more generally about marketing, if you want to grow the business more quickly you could look out for small firms with bright ideas that you might be able to acquire. Always choose items that are for a growing market and avoid anything to do with falling markets. In naming your product choose a short name that will look good when written in large lettering. Also it should be easy to say.

Price is important in helping to establish and secure business, and in difficult times a slight reduction in the price can do more than would be achieved by increasing the advertising. But, do not make the mistake of starting to think that price is the only consideration, for many other things can influence demand, such as changing habits, improved standard of living, perceived quality, and of course advertising and packaging.

It is not always a reduction in price that will bring about an improvement in sales. It might be better to improve quality, or advertising, packaging or point-of-sale inducements.

Keep in mind the size of the market you are entering. What is a reasonable market share to try and attain and sustain? Your share of the total market informs your sales forecast and a growing market is bound therefore to bring increased sales. You can then afford to spend more on advertising and promotion, which would still be a lower percentage of turnover, and you will be increasing profits. A bigger market share might mean that you could give a bigger margin to traders or perhaps even reduce the price slightly.

- No manager should ever be satisfied. With competition from rivals it is important to be striving constantly for improvement.

Know your enemy. Try not to be taken by surprise. Never stop looking for a better way to do everything. Especially try and improve methods of selling and distribution. Do not put all your thinking time into production methods and the savings you can make. It is no good having the prettiest product at a good price if nobody is buying it.

Bear in mind that technology is taking massive strides and methods soon become out of date. Look to cut costs that are not essential and try and find better ways of providing a service. Find good thinkers who can make improvements while sticking to the overall plan.

Selling and sales psychology is so important, and it is sales people who are keeping the factories running. That is why sales directors and managers earn such high salaries, often based on commission related to sales performance. Successful selling can turn a tidy business into a large concern. Any manager who underrates the value of the sales force is likely to be riding for a fall.

- If you can sell you will never starve.

Salesmanship can be the best-paid career in the world. A really good sales person is irreplacable. A manager could be replaced with not too much difficulty but a really super sales person is beyond price. No manager should be afraid to pay sales people well, and it is far from ridiculous that a good sales person should earn more than his or her employer. Their worth to the business has to be reflected in what they earn.

The good sales person knows that a customer has to want what is being offered. A customer therefore has to be made to realise that your product will either make, or save, money. The best time for a sales person to get a good order is when he or she has just got one!

Sales people need to be well educated, and a company will benefit from any efforts to make their sales staff better educated. Good sales people love selling and do not want to do anything else. The successful businessman recognises that salesmanship is a full-time partner in economic progress. For there to be satisfactory profits there is a constant balancing act to be achieved with product costs, expenses and revenue and the efforts of sales staff to increase sales while keeping expenses low will ensure the balance is maintained.

It is important that anyone who sells should be friendly and can make the customer feel important. Engaging in conversation should not mean delivering a monologue. Anyone who does not like people is unlikely to be any good at selling.

The main characteristics of a really successful sales person are:

- Likes people and shows it.

- Is enthusiastic.

- Is aggressive but not overly so.

- Has staying power.

- Is persuasive and persistent.

- Is willing to work hard consistently.

- Carefully plans the presentation.

- Always expects an order.

- Is loyal to the company and its management.

- Is ambitious for self and company.

- Is friendly and good natured.

- Inspires confidence and is convincing.

- Is always courteous and patient.

- Makes good use of time.

- Is generous in nature.

- Is always considerate of others.

- Is honest and trustworthy.

It is worth remembering that, other things being equal, a customer would rather buy from someone he or she likes and gets on with, than from someone who is not so well regarded.

- It is worth making the effort to train sales staff and help to bring out the best of their natural characteristics and abilities.

We have already considered that managers should never be satisfied, and this is especially the case with regard to turnover. If improvement of turnover is to be continual, all new ideas should be welcomed and the manager should have a curious nature that increases wisdom resulting from observation and experience.

Carnegie said that when he had finished a job of work he had no reserves. In other words he threw all that he had into his work. Such people are seldom defeated.

- A sales or marketing manager looking for success has to be exceptional. There will be no clock watching but rather a willingness to work all hours on all days.

"Anything for a quiet life" is not a maxim for management, for it is energy and enthusiasm that are the hallmarks of a successful business enterprise. Some of the best paid and most able managers turn up at work before anyone else and are still there when late arrivals have gone home. They agree with Thackery's view that it is "business first, pleasure afterwards".

It is worth repeating how important sales are to a business. C H Schwab said that "nothing has value until it has been demonstrated that it can be sold" and B C Forbes claimed that "success is largely salesmanship".

Intelligent marketing is equally vital to business success

and it is worthwhile to rehearse repeatedly what makes your preparation and presentation likely to succeed. You have to be sure you have covered all these tasks:

- Planning of the product range
- Well thought out pricing decisions
- Brand names
- Distribution channels
- Briefing of sales staff
- Advertising and promotion campaign
- Packaging
- Decision on selling to wholesalers, retailers or direct.

There is a need for definite and clear cut objectives:

- Aim for a certain market standing
- Encourage constant efforts to come up with new ideas.
- Secure a level of productivity
- Ensure there is sufficient finance
- Keep in mind a reasonable level of profit.

Marketing budgets need to consider the overall aspects of the business because it is quite possible for sales to be rising while the business is sinking. This can easily happen if margins are insufficient to cover all the costs. You could reach a situation where the more of the product you sell the more money you lose!

- The share of a market that a business attains is vital to survival. If market share in normal times is too small the business is likely to fail in hard times.

Let's say again and list the recurring themes of this chapter:

- Sales are the life blood of a business.
- Success is largely salesmanship.
- Handling people successfully is salesmanship.
- Not enough sales will lead to the death of the business.
- Orders maintain the life of the business.
- Customers make a business.
- 'No customer' is synonymous with 'no business'.
- Salesmanship includes the study of people.
- Salesmanship is getting on with all kinds of people.
- The successful sales person is welcomed by the buyer.
- The price must be right.
- The product must be attractively packaged.

Salesmanship is an excellent career and someone who can really sell will always have a job. Sales people are born not made, but to be really good it is necessary to study to improve sales techniques.

Basically, the personality has to be right. It is a very fulfilling career for those who are ideally suited to it. The real art is to demonstrate the product so well that you make a permanent customer.

Some sales people will say they do not have customers, only friends. Really confident sales people do not look for security but for opportunity. Dress, manner of speaking, attitude to people and the job, all have to be right.

If the sales manager has engaged the right people in the sales team, it is vital then to provide the incentives that will have the team working at its highest capabilities. If the marketing strategy is right, and there has been no underestimating of the opposition, there is no reason why the sales team cannot go out and achieve the targets.

9

PRACTICAL BUSINESS
PSYCHOLOGY

To study to learn is cheaper and quicker than to learn from experience, and it is less painful. Above all else, a manager must get on well with people and learn how to handle people. The application of psychology helps to check experiences of business and life and helps us to understand what makes people tick and how to make them tick more advantageously.

There are many studies of the products that people make. Business psychology is the study of people that make and buy the products.

- You only learn about people by studying people.

It is not sufficient for a would-be successful manager to simply guess about people. Many things are said and believed that a little enquiry will show are not true. Any manager basing his or her outlook on such misleading sayings will be unable to succeed at managing people.

It has often been said that sales are helped by pricing in round figures. This has been proved wrong so many times that it is a wonder it still circulates. An item priced at £100 will not necessarily sell better than if priced at £99.50. Actually, the reverse is more likely to be true.

It has been said of many who pose as trainers of businessmen that the fear of the sack is the best way to make people work hard. It may be one of the ways, as is apparent during times of recession. However, loyalty is often inspired by fair treatment. People respond to friendliness and they like to work for a firm of which they can be proud. The loyalty of staff to a good employer has often been demonstrated and the fear of dismissal has not featured in the reasons for their loyalty.

An often repeated assertion about advertising is that more men than women pay attention to an advertisement featuring a pretty girl. In fact, the opposite is true.

When I was learning how to judge people, wiseacres of the day told me that people would not be able to look me in the eye if lying to me. Obviously, for a liar to succeed he must inspire confidence, and looking you in the eye may well be part of the confidence inspiring technique.

- To be a successful manager it is essential to question what you are told.

Accept nothing as gospel unless it is borne out by experience. It must be understood that just because something is widely held to be true, it is no guarantee of its authenticity.

If you wish to believe what you are told then only listen to the views of successful people, and only then when they talk of their own field of experience. Once speaking outside their own experience even the wisest seem to fall for half truths and unsupported theories.

- Psychology will teach you that many people **believe only** what they want to believe.

This often reassures them in their non-proven bigotry. You must be completely honest with yourself if you are to understand others. Untruths do not become truths by being frequently repeated just as facts do not cease to be facts because they are ignored.

If you are to succeed as a leader (for leading is what a manager does) you must not accept anything you are told without trying to verify it. Study to find proof of a theory in the observed lives of those around you. Psychology deals with people.

- A manager cannot afford to be so busy that there is no time to think.

Bustling is not synonymous with working well. It may well be working badly. A truly busy person always has time to think. If, in your work, you do not allow time to think you will probably fail. Business psychology is not comfortable. It will often advance thoughts you do not want to accept. To be psychologically sound you must accept facts. It does not matter if the facts support your beliefs or not. You may find you are believing something that will keep you in bondage to a supposed fact while keeping you ignorant of the actual fact.

- A manager must act only in accordance with the facts.

Beliefs do not matter unless they are based on facts. Do not be diverted to an easier way. The correct way is the only sound way.

- To become a good manager of people you must be interested yourself in people.

You must study their abilities and their shortcomings. There must be a burning desire to improve people and to help them to be better equipped for whatever they wish to do.

A manager needs to like people and be capable of understanding their personalities and latent abilities despite any weaknesses. You may have noticed how much more someone can get out of a person compared with someone else; how a failure under one management can be a success under another.

It is said of George Washington that he made certain rules for himself from the age of 15. He held that it would be wrong to jog the desk of another writer. He believed it would be wrong to be pleased at the misfortune of another, even one much disliked. He held that when a man did all he could and yet failed, he should not be blamed. He held that in expressing reproof, no anger should be shown. He felt that reports against others should only be accepted with care; that the blemishes of others should not be stressed.

It must be difficult to consider people psychologically while holding a grudge against them, because psychology is constructive not destructive. The psychological ideal is to bring out the best in others.

The psychological outlook is a way of regarding people with understanding, and not simply as good or bad. People should be observed as they are. Then they can be measured.

- Seek to bring out the best in others.

No trickery is needed. Forget thoughts about good or bad. Observe people as they are and do not jump to conclusions. A manager should be self schooled to observe with the intention of learning the facts about every individual. Looking back is not a good way of observing. You can have opinions, provided you do not regard them as facts.

Opinions are not facts. A manager should constantly search for facts. New facts.

It is acceptable to admit that you do not know about someone, so long as you go on searching for the facts. Psychological facts help you to put the right person in the right job. Psychology does not replace work but can make work easier. It can increase skill in performance. It can help you to get on well with other people. It can improve personal health, both physical and mental.

A psychological outlook can improve personal resources. Many people only use part of their potential powers. They could make fuller use of their abilities. The question is, how can the job be done more easily or better. It saves time to do the job right the first time without hang ups that have to be overcome.

- Aim to get better results, more often, with less effort.

Improve your personal efficiency. It is quite possible to be a spendthrift of time and energy. Clothes can be bought for look and not for long-wearing qualities. One can buy a flashy rather than an economical car.

- Fast action is no substitute for planned efficiency.

Work out a business system that cuts out useless and wearying activities. Consider carefully what efficiency means.

Study the ratio between input and output. To be efficient does not mean working at top speed until you collapse. We have already thought about how important it is to make time to think.

Do a reasonable amount of work with less exhausting effort. A scientific outlook is to comprehend the relationship between energy used and results achieved.

- The genuinely busy person always seems to have time, is calm and unharassed.

Applied to business this means that efficiency is the relationship between wages paid and output achieved, or between expenditure and receipts.

It is easier to push than to pull a heavy load. Efficiency means that strain is kept to a minimum.

It is important for management to realise that there is a loss of personal efficiency if an individual who is capable of being an accountant, is instead efficiently running a photocopying machine. Unused talent is a loss of efficiency. Wasted potential is a management crime. Try to upgrade your staff all the time. It is always possible for work procedures to seek the lowest level, like water. A pump is needed to correct the adverse flow. The pump is the motivation applied by an expert manager.

Staff can be working in a low gear unintentionally, gradually losing efficiency and reaching a kind of creeping paralysis. Personal efficiency dies at this point. When the lower level of work becomes the norm it becomes stereotyped.

Make for yourself a quota of efficiency. Work towards a goal. If you have a goal you will tend to make better use of your abilities. Set the goal yourself, and do not set it too high. Make it a reachable goal.

- To set a goal too high is in itself inefficiency because it causes unnecessary stress.

Boredom and wear and tear on the spirit are part of the unseen input of a job, the rarely calculated overhead. Strain is always inefficient. From time to time work hard at nothing. Enjoy a little pleasure in the middle of serious work. Work for a dream without making it into a nightmare. Take your work in your stride, without unnecessary strain and inner conflict.

Make your abilities effective in what you achieve. Concentrate on achievement.

- If you have not learned to concentrate you will not be efficient.

Concentration assists in learning, improves memory, and advances rational thought. Output is speeded by concentration. Errors arise from lack of concentration. For example, when driving a car, lack of concentration can have dire results.

Concentration is the focus of the mind. Concentration on something makes it vivid and other surrounding things become vague. Just as you need to focus to get a good photograph you need to concentrate to achieve good work.

You must always be concentrating on something. Make sure your concentration is directed towards accomplishing your aims. Do not get the central point out of focus. Keep the focus steady until the photograph has been taken. Keep the concentration until the task has been completed. Concentration needs staying power without which efficiency is not possible.

- Staying power and clarity of vision are hallmarks of the well adjusted mind.

Concentration increases over a short time to reach maximum output. Start work energetically to reduce the time to reach full concentration.

Efforts must be made to retain the concentration of others. When talking to someone their attention is apt to lapse every so often. When selling, for instance, attention can be regained by changing the tone of your voice, or by asking a question. To move around helps to hold the attention of the other person.

Believe in yourself. Believe you can concentrate. You can always concentrate better. Rapid workers concentrate best.

- You will concentrate better if you believe in yourself.

There are hindrances to concentration. A desk beside a window invites lack of concentation and wool-gathering. Interruptions need not block concentration. Give only a very small part of your mind to the interruption. Think more about the job in hand and less about the interruption.

When concentrating on some work do not let anything interrupt. Do not fiddle nor even smoke. Plan work so that work of the same kind is done in batches. Make all phone calls together. Do all mathematical work in one batch.

A manager who has learned to concentrate is then able to teach concentration to others. Daydreaming is the enemy of concentration and is a sign that you do not enjoy your work. Such daydreaming tends towards accidents and mistakes. Do not indulge in random thinking.

As suggested earlier, it is easier if you aim at a goal. You will not use your mind aimlessly if you have a goal to work towards. Working to a deadline aids concentration. When concentrating on a new job, aim at complete accuracy right from the start.

- Keep your workplace for concentrating on work.
  Relax somewhere else.

Moneymaking ideas can be gleaned from reading. Thomas Edison said that when he wanted to invent something he began by reading eveything written on the subject. He said that he used these books to prevent waste of time or money, by not repeating what had already been done by others. In his early days Henry Ford spent every penny he could on books.

- Those who want to be good managers must read a lot, and seriously.

In reading, the aim is to grasp the meaning quickly. The proficient reader is a fast reader. Read for the meaning. Read with the head not with the lips. To concentrate in reading take in an entire phrase at a glance. Read phrases not words. Catch meanings quickly. Most people could read twice as much in the same time, if they taught themselves to read properly. More time does not equate to more reading.

Word fluency is essential to a good manager, as well as in solving crossword puzzles. Word fluency makes dictation smooth and without hesitation. A good communicator can use fewer words because every word counts.

Read for a purpose. Build an efficient memory. Memory is an activity. Everyone has the power of remembering. Concentrate on making memory intentional. Keep it exercised. Anything not worth remembering should be dispensed with immediately. Memory improves with use.

It is important for a manager to be proficient in the attitude and skills that he or she wants to teach to others. That is why it is so important to work at concentration and memory training. The would-be successful manager must want to learn. The good and successful manager needs a wide and general knowledge.

- Those who would teach must learn.

To learn efficiently you must unlearn errors by giving them unpleasant associations. Know why. Study, reading and reasoning help to gain knowledge. Go for accuracy because accuracy will lead to speed in learning.

Let's think about a few simple statements to do with learning:

- It is better to try oneself than to watch others.
- The best teacher in the world is the effort to learn.
- Make learning a game.
- Learning is more effective when it is fun.
- You are what you have learned.
- Widen your skills and increase your worth.
- Good learners are good earners.
- Read to become a more influential person.
- Learn from those who are better than you.
- View your business as a whole.
- What you want is business sense.
- Develop continuously.
- Never be complacent.
- Constantly exercise the mind.
- Overcome the reluctance to learn more.
- Do not refuse new knowledge.
- The new keeps business going.
- Once you refuse to learn you are too old to learn.

Most people could learn more if they tried. Leading and reading are companions. Make the effort to read more non-fiction. If you are curious you will look forward to change and new methods. Those who know the most are often eager to learn more, and best able to do so. Keep learning, for the world moves on but habitual learners move with it.

Be expectant. Aiming at goals means expectant behaviour. Expectancy means optimism.

We have already given thought to the importance of dealing with interruptions. They are a hindrance and get in the way of concentration. You must make sure you stick to business during business hours, and concentrate only on essentials. Climb mountains not molehills and do nothing that does not need doing. Do not worry about frills.

- Do not start lots and finish little.

Work at ease and show a relaxed attitude to work. Relaxed working is not lazy working. Unhurried thoroughness is speed in the long run. The efficient person makes effort appear invisible.

One thing the able manager must do well is match people with jobs. People differ in different ways and it is important to understand this and to appreciate how their abilities and prospects will be affected by doing different jobs.

To be average is to be between fast and slow and it must be remembered that it is in this category that most people will be found. In the chapter on staff selection we considered that training does not iron out differences but tends to increase them. It is important to remember that whoever is best at a certain job after one week is likely still to be best after one year.

People have preferences and interests and these tend to suggest a likely and successful career. I have always believed that people will work best at doing what they like to do.

There is nothing as sad as the sight of a man or woman

who is utterly weary every day after working at something he or she hates.

The wise applicant for a job will be pleased to take psychological tests as this is likely to place them in a job most suited to their abilities. Managers should make all applicants feel at home and should treat them in a conversational manner. A conversation can turn to discovering information about experience, training, habits, interests and aptitudes.

- Always let the interviewee do the greater part of the talking.

It is important to get across to any job applicant a good impression of the company and its standing. Keep the atmosphere friendly and try and get on good terms from the start. Build a good human relationship. If you do this it will bear fruit in helpfulness and loyalty. Remember the applicant's early opinion of the company will be based on that first interview with you.

It is important to get along in all human relationships, not just at work but at home and at leisure. Do not evade problems in any part of your life for it can lead to the same attitude at work.

Never be negative. Do whatever you can to make relationships positive or they may remain negative. What you fail to do that you should do may be as disastrous as doing the wrong things.

- Remember that people matter and are far more important than machines.

Treat everyone as you would like to be treated. You will get back what you give, often with interest. Some people will prove hard to get on with. Try to discover why.

- Your best employees will be found among those with
  a zest for living.

People with a zest for living will find their work worth doing and will enjoy making a success of the work they do. They believe in themselves, and will be out to prove themselves in all that they do. High morale makes a worker unbeatable.

A man or woman with good morale has adjusted to life and is at harmony with the world. The secret of happiness has been found in all sectors of this person's life. He or she will work well and will influence others positively.

This person will be optimistic and has no time for pessimistic thought. He or she is an inspiration to others. Such people individually and in groups believe in their company and its aims and have tremendous company pride.

Managers, and bosses generally, should remember that people like to feel needed. They also like to feel their interests have been catered for. Do all you can in the way of friendly interest in your workers' health, recreation and progress in the company.

- Remember a caring boss can do more good than
  the best working conditions.

Managers must take an interest in their staff because a job is not only a living it is a way of life. If you have good lighting in your office, make sure your workers have the same. The canteen should be a place fit to eat and relax in and should be shared as far as possible with management and staff together.

If you fail to appreciate your staff as people, no amount of money will make them happy. Be observant. Appreciate people. Notice them and help them. Compliment staff on work well done, especially on good orders taken.

Empathy is an appreciation of what lies behind another's thoughts and actions. Empathy is appreciation and understanding. A compulsive drinker is best helped by Alcoholics Anonymous because they are people who understand the problems faced by, and can empathise with, someone with a drink problem.

- The person who has empathy can understand the viewpoint of others.

It is an intellectual understanding and helps with an appreciation of the behaviour of another person. Experience and observation will increase one's level of empathy. It pays to observe and learn.

- It is not difficult for a manager to judge success in building up a good and contented workforce.

Do they keep good hours and look happy at work? Is morale good? If there is absenteeism and high staff turnover, then it is certain that morale is low. Are there many trivial complaints from workers? It is a sign that something is wrong in the business.

Make sure that all workers, even the part-time cleaner, can take pride in their work. Upgrading is good as it makes a job more socially desirable. Shorter working hours and more money will not replace a feeling that the work done is worthwhile and respected by the management.

People wish to be well thought of and workers who feel that you think well of them will want to please you. A manager should constantly feed self regard. If you believe someone is capable of doing something and you show this belief, you will probably find they can do it.

People really do care how they are treated. Office morale should be maintained at all times and the mood of the manager must not interfere with this morale.

A happy workforce is one that:

- Is well informed
- Feels secure
- Is given a feeling of individual dignity
- Is complimented on good work
- Is fairly paid
- Feels important and needed.

People must feel important to take a pride in their work. Information is vital. There is usually less industrial trouble in offices than in factories. This is in part due to the tendency for office workers to know more about the business than workers on the shop floor.

Managers should always use words that compliment and build self esteem. They should never hurt feelings or belittle members of staff.

The most likely way to gain a person's co-operation is to build their self esteem. You will always be liked if you help others to like themselves. Help the other fellow to blow his horn.

Give the best possible title to a job and that will increase morale. If you lift you can lead. No member of staff will look up at a boss who looks down on him or her. Laugh with people and certainly not at them. A hint is always better than an order.

Never be condescending. Instead, build people up and let your own abilities and accomplishments speak for themselves.

You will either make friends of have enemies. Let people

feel they are working with you rather than for you. Let them share in success.

- Make your staff ambitious by example.

Paranoid people believe that they have to fight for their rights all the time. Avoid such people if you can. Offer friendliness and you will probably get friendliness back.

- If you do not show friendliness you will receive hostility.

Some parents never do anything really bad to their children, yet they do not have their affection. The same lack of friendliness is probably the reason why some managers find that their staff would cheerfully wring their necks. Friendliness has to be a positive thing. Keep in touch with staff.

A manager has to notice when things are going well or the staff will not pull together with him or her when times are difficult. The silent treatment may be right in a prison but not in a business relationship.

The personal touch has high value. Know and remember the names of all employees. An individual relationship will lead to better work and unsolicited loyalty.

Every business should be a friendly place to work. Be easy to know and talk to. Those you notice will notice you. Greetings should be heartfelt and human not mechanical. Really look at people. Be skilled in the art of knowing and liking people. Show an interest in their work, their clothes, their car, their family. Aim to like more people. Try to like them soon after they join your workforce. Tell them.

People respond to encouragement. Discouragement is the enemy of high morale. A discouraged worker will probably be a bad worker. To encourage is to inspire and give hope of a great future. It costs so little to achieve so much.

Give all the encouragement you can to a new worker, or at the beginning of a new venture, and after a promotion. Remember that what you tell a person they can do they probably will do.

Tell a beginner he or she has made a good beginning. Inculcate a positive frame of mind in each worker, and maintain it with congratulations and promote whenever possible. Never fail to give credit but do not take it yourself. To give credit to staff for work well done is to prove your own competence to manage.

- Do not send an expert to teach a beginner, rather use an average worker to do the teaching.

The learner will feel more at ease and the average worker will be the better for teaching and for feeling that he or she is held in sufficient esteem to be trusted with this important task.

- Be encouraging when someone has a bad day.

We all have bad days at some time or other. When having a bad day a worker will expect things to go wrong. Encourage this person to believe this will not be so. Encouragement brings out the best in people.

Make sure you are not the kind of manager who appears only when something has gone wrong. Be there always to praise good work and celebrate good results. A sales person should compliment the customer. It is surprising how people expand when praised. Such praise should be definite not vague. It is well proven that praise is more likely to get results than criticism. To give hope is to spur.

- Optimism is catching but so is pessimism.

Be sure which prevails in your company. It is undoubtedly

the fault of management if the staff are pessimistic.

Look for good points in your workers remembering that the most certain way to fail in human relationships is to be constantly emphasising faults. You must handle others with the objective of bringing out the best. You must look for the best in order to do this. Make a habit of looking for good things. Some people comment on the bird song every morning, others only see the rain.

Personality tells in management. Be sure to cultivate your whole personality. This includes pleasantness, ambition, initiative, responsibility and diligence. Your personality is your style of life. Personality shows at all times. It is your quality of life.

- Your personality will show in your walk. It can show confidence, timidity, carelessness, precision, enthusiasm or laziness. Walk sure.

Customers in a store will tend to approach the smart and not the slovenly among the assistants. Dress and look well.

A good disposition lasts better than a pretty face. Employ the people of good disposition. If they are good looking as well that is a bonus, but however pretty, a sour disposition will only have negative results in a business.

It is a fact that people may not be all that they seem. A good secretary may also be a silly flirt. A cruel prison warder may be a kind and caring husband. The path between extremes is to be aimed at. To develop a rounded and sympathetic personality likely to inspire success in life, you should practise mental exaltation at taking on any job. Feel pleasure and sorrow and the whole gamut of emotions. Feel with others.

At an early age every person should cultivate the personality traits to best serve his or her career. Form good habits. Practice will make perfect if you practise the best habits.

Try to be intelligent, cheerful, friendly, helpful, generous, loyal, honest, sincere, and always with a sense of humour.

Try to avoid the traits that make for a sour personality, such as intemperate, critical, sarcastic, boastful, cheating and avoid cultivating an affected manner.

As it is easier to add new qualities than it is to lose undesirable ones, focus on the positive. Add desirable new habits. Drop unwanted traits by taking up the opposite good habits.

Work out for yourself the personality you wish to cultivate. Associate with people with personalities you feel are worth copying. Look up to great men and great things. Carlisle said, "Show me the man you honour and I will show you the kind of man you are."

- In a new job the recruit may feel lonely. Appoint a trusted worker to look after someone new.

The new worker will be able to build relationships by being friendly and getting to know new people each day, and by being encouraged to ask colleagues for help.

Get rid of frustrations by desiring what can be done. A balanced personality means successfully taking life as it is. Adjust your attitude to life and be free of frustrations.

- Make a list of your ambitions in life.

Discard the unattainable and forget about them. Decide what you can get on without, and make the very best of what you can attain.

Nervous tension should be avoided. If wound up too tightly, people become anxious and restless, and little problems seem huge. They squander energy and exaggerate their troubles. Inside themselves they carry the germs of frustration. Their desire for success is greater than their satisfaction with the successes they have achieved.

A good manager can help the frustrated to get rid of their frustrations by recognising the signs.

The most obvious signs of frustration are:

- Antagonism
- Nagging
- Anti-social attitudes
- Bullying
- Laziness
- Gossiping
- Chip on the shoulder
- Rigidity
- A closed mind
- Giving up.

In life the adjusted person knows he or she must give and take. To take continually, leads to frustration.

Emotional tension is of the mind, but it can have profound effects on the body. For instance, anger makes the face flush, and can be the cause of an ulcer. High blood pressure can be a result of built up tension. Many vital physical processes can be affected by emotions. The mind affects the body much more than the body affects the mind.

There is a high-blood-pressure personality that comes out as resentment of authority. It is not hard work that kills.

Sometimes, ulcers come to people who craved for but did

not get affection and approval in early life. Lack of affection can bring on feelings of failure. This feeling lingers and in adult life leads to a striving for success. The underlying sourness within, against the world in general, can be the start of an ulcer. Success will bring an improvement in the condition, failure makes it worse.

Heart attacks are often brought on by fear or anxiety. Striving over mightily for success can lead to coronary trouble.

- Bodily health depends much on a person's attitude and personality.

Mental illnesses are just as painful as those caused by poisons. Ideas and attitudes are very powerful influences on life.

- Emotional maturity is essential to business success.

Life starts with total dependence. Some continue to lean on others forever. When one first toddles there is bewilderment. This stage is quickly followed by showing off, the "watch me" phase. Correction by parents results in stamping and screaming against the authority. Often the child will bite or sulk. Then he or she will go through a stage of being very stubborn. As the child grows older it will join a group or gang of friends. At puberty the gang is abandoned as interest is shown in the opposite sex. This should then be followed by mature independence. Plans are made for a career, a family, provision for old age, etc. One becomes a responsible and caring citizen. This screaming, sulking, stubborn child has grown up to be a calm and tolerant adult.

The adult person now has a long range plan, and is no longer affected by the whims and changing desires of each passing week. He or she is now much more interested in the future than in the past. There is no longer a need to show off to boost confidence, no nursed grudges, and unpleasant tasks are now tackled without self pity. This person can now take orders and is capable of making decisions. Friends are from both sexes. Criticism is accepted and benefit comes from it.

It can be said that the person has come of age emotionally, and has acquired new personality habits and emotional attitudes. The clowning of a four year old will not suit a 24 year old. A teenager may giggle at anything and everything, may be tardy and have fads, but none of this is right for a mature person.

Insight is the key to changing personality. To help others the manager must have this insight, because self understanding brings emotional release. The best way to help others to reach this self knowledge is to let them talk about themselves until the vague inner feelings are being expressed in words. Telling a person what to do is useless. Listening will help. The person will hand you the key to their personality.

Good leadership is worth millions. The wrong type of leadership will lead to absenteeism and dissatisfaction. Even the most generous piece rates will not produce a good output under a tyrant. Lead rather than drive for the best results.

Rockefeller said that he would pay more for the ability to handle men than for any other ability.

Running a business is a group effort. Planning is needed. Someone must do the planning. Developing skills is the leader's job. Most people wish to be led.

Why do some firms suffer more strikes than others? Some workers are faced with threats of punishment for offences against the rules. Others are offered rewards for cooperation. Leadership by teaching and explaining will still produce the results when the boss has looked away. Better still is leadership by inspiration. This is creative. Inspiring leaders offer rewards, give encouragement, listen, keep informed and explain how and why.

- The creative leader builds a group spirit of teamwork and it is often not necessary to give orders.

People will accept the leadership of those whose ability they respect. They give loyalty in return for consideration.
   Leaders must get things done. They must keep the costs down and must build group spirit. Leaders need knowledge, planning judgement and, above all, a knack with people.

- Inability to get on with people contributes more to failures than lack of specialised knowlege.

Executives are to be judged by:

- Ability to make decisions
- Sensitivity
- Personality
- Fairness
- Integrity
- Energy
- Ability to teach.

To show that you have personal leadership you must:

- Look successful
- Keep mentally alert
- Be stimulating.

A leader needs followers. People like to be led but this should not be abused.

Your level of knowledge helps to give force to leadership. Power accompanies those who know what has to be done. Other powerful people follow a good leader. Good leaders surround themselves with people who know more than they do. They learn from them.

A good leader is never ashamed to ask for information because there is always the desire to learn more and increase power. Knowledge is power.

- Have capable assistants who will push you up and follow you up.

The leader must find out what needs doing, determine the way to do it, then inspire others to do it. A strong personality makes this persuasion easy. A hint from a powerful leader is better than an order from a poor one.

People are choosy about who they will follow. Not all are content to be led. Liking for the leader arises from the leader's personal qualities. With great knowledge and strong personality a leader is born.

There are many traits of a leader's character that will show:

- Good at organising
- Respectful of others' feelings
- A genuine liking for people
- Fighting to get own way
- Does not have moods
- Is clearly popular
- Knows how to mix socially

- Has good judgement
- Shows persistence to overcome obstacles
- Is ambitious with a desire to excel
- Is good humoured
- Fun to work with
- Lively and intelligent.

The great leader also has originality, and a hallmark is the self confidence that inspires others. Leadership has to be learned and improved. Learn to lead naturally and without bossiness. Lead people to decide for themselves, remembering that people co-operate best when they are actively involved.

A leader will demonstrate constructive emotions like:

- Joy and Wonder
- Affection and Pity
- Cheerfulness and Laughter.

Constructive emotions spring from inner peace of mind. Destructive emotions come from inner tensions.

- Tender emotions are powerful.

That is why people with only fair abilities, but who are likeable, make good leaders and better salesmen than many more brilliant people. The very best sales people lead their prospects to talk themselves into buying. All leaders help people to make up their minds. Decision leads to action. Impel not compel is the watchword of successful leaders.

Develop impelling leadership. Discuss possible changes with the person who will be affected by them and encourage discussion and comment. You will see that this will make the other person feel important and increase confidence in you. Treat others as seed beds for ideas. Plant ideas in their minds. The measure of one's ability as a leader is to get others to see what needs to be done, and to do it.

The leader should leave him or her self open to be imitated. The leader must originate the action for others to copy. A growing trend seems to be an excess of meetings which are often too long. Meetings need to have a useful outcome or they become a waste of time.

The way you conduct your meetings will be imitated so make sure your leadership is good. You need to plan well ahead, arrange what is to happen, carry out what is decided. Give credit and make people feel involved. The company must be their company.

The good salesman makes the most awkward customer feel the most delightful person. The impeller can get things done without saying a word by providing the example to imitate.

The impelling voice shows:

- Enthusiasm
- Confidence
- Pleasantness.

The impelling leader:

- Arouses constructive emotions
- Guides others to decide
- Gives credit
- Plants ideas

- Shares responsibility
- Remains likeable
- Considers others.

Under a good manager people become proud to work where they do. Group feelings of pride assists production. Do not allow group conflicts to arise. Gossip and intolerance arise from prejudice and must be avoided. Provide people with a goal to work towards and give them something to look forward to. Have a philosophy.

Offer goals such as:
- Reducing accidents
- Reducing waste
- Increasing quality
- Improving the product
- Reducing absenteeism
- Steady employment.

Management should set good examples in hard times. Much criticism has been levelled at directors who accept large pay increases for themselves during a recession. Industrial relations suffer when such action coincides with redundancies. These are times when management must give a lead.

Finally, I would like to finish this chapter on practical business psychology with the words of Emerson:

'He who has a thousand friends, has not a friend to spare,

And he who has one enemy will meet him everywhere.'

10

SUMMARY BY SLOGAN

In reading this book you will have realised, if you didn't already, that being a successful businessman requires far more than just having a special ability in a certain field. There is so much to concentrate on that it becomes hard to focus at times.

Improvement comes little by little. It may help if you pick a few apt slogans, make a copy of them and leave them where you can see them often. Work away at improving certain things until you do them without thinking. That way you will be doing all you can to bring success into whatever area of business you have chosen to work in. Good luck!

Learning by experience is the most costly way of learning.

No new business can afford to increase prices too soon.

There is no substitute for thorough preparation.

Any fool can give his goods away.

Profits must cover <u>all</u> expenses.

There is no substitute for knowledge.

A look at the stock will tell you if the buying has been competent.

The assets of a business may not be worth what they cost.

Goodwill is only of value if it has future benefit.

If it is going to be difficult or if it will take a long time to make any kind of profit from the business, then the buying price must be low.

It may be that turnover has been achieved at too high a cost.

There is no substitute for facts.

There is no worse enemy of yourself or your creditors than the official receiver.

Never say die until dead.

The best use of the money available is the art of good management.

No good is no good however low the cost might be.

The first law of modern business is survival.

Good organisation is growth resulting from the co-ordination of all the activities of a business.

Cause and effect applies as much in business as it does in nature.

There is considerable pleasure and fulfilment in running your own business.

It is important that a partner should be chosen carefully.

All business involves risk taking.

Most businesses do not make a profit.

One of the most needed aspects of management is the ability to bring out the best in others.

If you do not deserve loyalty you do not get loyalty.

Enthusiasm is catching.

Staff want to believe in what they are doing.

You must have money to survive.

You do not have to fail.

In most situations in life there is room for
improvement.

A constant check should be kept on all
aspects of a business.

Stagnation is death.

Encourage initiative in all.

Aim at authority without injustice.

The business with the least efficient
management is the business likely to be
subject to the most fraud.

Without sales there will be no funds for
anything else.

No money is wasted by a good manager.

A good manager has to inspire others.

The overriding purpose of a business is to make and keep customers.

Profits are the ultimate test of business efficiency.

No business can live forever on past achievements.

Innovation will keep customers interested.

How much is done that is not necessary?

A manager successfully directing events will prevent emergencies arising.

The person who matters is the customer.

No business can stand still.

Treat customers as friends.

Good staff relations will produce good customer relations.

You cannot plan for profit without planning for cost.

Unnecessary work of any kind should be avoided.

Do what is necessary and do nothing that has no purpose.

It is worthwhile to help your customer to pay your bill.

All staff must take holidays.

The employee is idle who could be doing something more taxing.

A diseased plant will not benefit from better soil.

Native abilities will not be altered by training.

Half a column of editorial is worth more than a page of advertising.

News is only news for a day.

Everything you say or write should do a sales job for your company.

It is the outstanding that captures the interest.

Make it easy for prospective customers to buy your product.

Advertising is wasteful if it fails to sell.

Advertising must be honest.

There is nothing evil in the promotion of desire.

Good managers enjoy the fight.

The battle to be the best is good for all.

Repetition is the hallmark of a successful advertising campaign.

Reputation grows naturally out of sound principles and good products.

If you do not sell your goods you do not have a business.

A pretty packet round an item that does not sell is a waste of money.

Management must make things happen.

Nothing worthwhile will be achieved without knowledge.

Often very good ideas fail because not enough attention is given to salesmanship.

Do not aim at a void.

Misunderstandings make enemies.

The only real reason for a retailer to stock
an item is in the expectation of selling it.

Advertising without adequate distribution
is a marketing crime.

Do not conclude that price is the only
consideration.

No manager should ever be satisfied.

Find good thinkers.

It is the sales people who keep the
factories running.

If someone can sell they will never starve.

Salesmanship is a full time partner in
economic progress.

Make the customer feel important.

A good sales person does like people.

Success means being an exception to the average.

"Anything for a quiet life" is not a maxim for good management.

Nothing has value until it has been demonstrated it can be sold.

It is possible for sales to rise while a business sinks.

Sales are the life blood of a business.

Success is largely salesmanship.

Customers make a business.

A sales person does not look for security but for opportunity.

A good sales person need not resort to trickery.

Competition has to be overcome not ignored.

To study to learn is cheaper than to learn by experience.

You only learn about people by studying people.

The fact that something is widely held to be true is no guarantee of its authenticity.

A great many people only believe what they want to believe.

Opinions are not facts.

The genuinely busy person always seems to have time.

Unused talent is a loss of efficiency.

Read for the meaning.

Memory improves with using.

You are what you have learned.

Your best employees will be found among those with a zest for living.

People like to feel needed.

A job is not only a living, it's also a way of life.

Make sure all the workers can take pride in their work.

You will always be liked if you help others to like themselves.

Build people up.

Be skilled in the art of knowing and liking people.

People respond to encouragement.

The manager should not be somebody who only appears when something goes wrong.

Walk sure.

A balanced personality means taking life as it is.

Mind affects body more than body affects mind.

Good leadership is worth millions.

Rockefeller said that he would pay more for the ability to handle men than for any other ability.

Business is a group effort.

Inability to get on with people contributes more to failures than lack of specialised knowledge.

A leader needs followers.

Leadership is something much more than bossiness.

Plant ideas.

Arrange what happens.

Under a good manager people become proud to work where they do.